MEGALIFE

Also by J. Marshall Craig

Between Rock and a Home Place

Don't Let Me Be Misunderstood

Scars & Strikes

Guilty By Association

Eh Mail

You're Lucky If You're Killed

Growing a Better America

MEGALIFE

THE AUTOBIOGRAPHY OF

Nick Menza

J. MARSHALL CRAIG

A POST HILL PRESS BOOK

Megalife:
The Autobiography of Nick Menza
Original work by J. Marshall Craig © Copyright 2018 J. Marshall Craig.
Original work by Nick Menza © Copyright 2018 Menzanation, LLC
All Rights Reserved

ISBN: 978-1-64293-049-8
ISBN (eBook): 978-1-64293-050-4

Cover design by Cody Corcoran
Interior design and composition, Greg Johnson, Textbook Perfect

Post Hill Press
New York · Nashville
posthillpress.com

Published in the United States of America

CONTENTS

Foreword: J. Marshall Craig vii

Introduction: Nick Menza xiii

A Heavy Drummer's Lighter Side xvii

Chapter One: "Just A Regular Gig" 1

Rim Shot: Losing Our Grip 32

Chapter Two: Mustaine Remains the Same 35

Rim Shot: Two Twenties for a Ten 47

Chapter Three: Little Drummer Boy 53

Rim Shot: A Bad Night in Eugene, Oregon 65

Chapter Four: North Hollywood High 67

Rim Shot: Tattoo You 79

Chapter Five: In My Life 80

Rim Shot: Random Acts of Danger 97

Chapter Six: "Will the Real Nick Menza Please Sit Down?" 101

Rim Shot: What's in a Name? 114

Chapter Seven: "I Pledge Allegiance…" 118

Rim Shot: Wouldn't You? 128

Chapter Eight: But Are They Illegal Aliens? 131

Rim Shot: Hit Rewind! 140

Chapter Nine: Hitting Things with Sticks 144

Rim Shot: Soap in My Eyes 154

Chapter Ten: Drum Worship 156

"That Terrible Night" 178

Last Word 190

Acknowledgments 194

Photo Credits 196

About the Author 198

FOREWORD

Ars longa, vita brevis.
(Art is long, life is short.)

This is not the book I wanted to write.

I set out with Nick Menza to help him write the wildly exciting story of his life both on and off the stage, as one of the best, most thunderous drummers in rock 'n' roll history—and one of the truly genuine souls one could ever meet. Indeed, that's the book we arrived at over the course of several years, progress made first with me accepting his unusual invitation to move into his Studio City home in a crash course effort for us to get to know each other deeply and quickly, and then with an untold number of phone calls, emails, texts, and visits back and forth across the county. Our last session was a weeklong getaway to Carpinteria, California, where I introduced him to a recording studio that I had been doing some film work in, and which desperately needed a new session drummer. It was to be our last time together. We certainly hadn't planned it that way. Nick had a ticket to fly to my home in Cape Cod on May 23, 2016 for our final interviews and writing sessions, and to brainstorm some of the ceaseless film, TV, and other book ideas we both had, among them an animated series and band he was calling "The Atomic Disintegrator."

Little more than twenty-four hours before his flight, Nick...left early. Certainly, tragically, years before anyone could possibly have imagined. He was playing at one of his favorite clubs with two of his favorite fellow musicians, Chris Poland and Robertino "Pag" Pagliari, in their band Ohm. The club is legendary, frequented for nearly the past half-century by fans and players as diverse as Clint Eastwood, Larry Carleton, Chad Smith of Red Hot Chili Peppers, and countless others. Barely three miles from Nick's house, I've joined untold fellow fans there in failing spectacularly to finish one of their namesake baked potatoes, which are generally, in my experience, larger than most people's feet. (Nick, incidentally, always finished his.)

On that day, May 21, however, sometime before midnight, Nick blazed through the first three songs of the opening set, almost challenging Chris and Pag to match his intensity. Chris smiled and shook his head at Nick as if to plead for some mercy. Pag looked back and winked, and Nick winked back at him with a smile. Just before they began the fourth song, Chris and Pag turned to look. Nick was leaned awkwardly against Pag's amp. Then he fell backwards. Chris yelled for 911, and an off-duty EMT was on the stage seconds later. An ambulance arrived within minutes and took over CPR, and for forty-something excruciating minutes EMTs tried everything to bring Nick back. But he was frozen forever from this world; he'd moved on, at the age of fifty-one, to his next big gig.

Nick's mother, Rose, also lives close to the club and made it there in time to touch her only son's hand before he was lifted into the ambulance. Nick, she told me tearfully at his private memorial less than a month later, felt cold; he was gone, and Rose knew it before anyone else.

Nick's sister Donia raced over to the club too, and she was there as paramedics were still working valiantly, to resuscitate him. His Dad, Don, was on tour in Germany and couldn't return until late the next day.

As for the story Nick and I were telling—you, me, his family and friends—we're the ones with an ending no one wanted. Nothing I nor anyone else can do about that. It's taken me a long, painful time to rewrite and amend what was a now-and-then glance back but more importantly what Nick so excitedly dreamt of to come.

I couldn't have done it without the support and encouragement of Nick's mom and dad, (Rose and Don), Donia, Nick's boys Nicholas and Donte, and their mom, Terri. Or, indeed, without the kindness and help from his many friends all over the world.

FOREWORD

One thing I couldn't bring myself to do was change the positive, wondrous tone of the man I knew well. In keeping with Nick's optimistic, almost boyish excitement of future promises for all of us, I've kept the tense of the book largely in the present. It seems to me that referring to Nick in the past is out of tune. Better to be with the joyous, astounding, and kindly comical spirit that is Nick—which leads me to a joke; one of the first things he ever said to me.

> An anthropologist is deep in the jungle studying a primitive tribe. One night, drums begin thundering in the distance. Worried, the scientist asks one of the tribal leaders, "What does that mean?"
>
> The native replies, "Drums OK...but if drums stop very bad...run away."
>
> The drums beat on for some time. The anthropologist, still ill at ease, asks again if there is any danger. The native repeats himself: "Drums OK...but if drums stop very bad...run away."
>
> After another hour, the drums stop. The native looks up and says, "Drums stop! Very bad! Run away!"
>
> The terrified anthropologist asks, "What happens next?"
>
> The native replies, "Bass solo!"

You may have heard that joke a million times (or not—I hadn't). But it was among Nick's favorites. And this is saying something, because Nick could just as easily have been a standup comic instead of the drummer for Megadeth, Ohm, and a half-dozen other bands. I believe now even more than I did upon meeting Nick: such a restrained, clever, outlandish wit I am unlikely to meet again. Who else would call up the local drum shop's poorly experienced staff and dryly ask if they still had any left-handed drum stools in stock? People have asked me if Nick actually sat down at a computer and wrote, or if he went out to his zen garden with pen and paper in hand and opened that metaphoric vein to let his soul spill out onto the pages. Well, no, that's why he called me. The best and most accurate way to describe this book is to say it's the alchemy of Nick's words and my writing, shaped by our years of friendship and my observations and experiences with him and his many dear friends and peers. We never worked full-time, so the research spanned several years, and then there was another year of writing after his shocking death based on hundreds of hours of interviews in his studio, drum room, kitchen, over the phone, Skype and emails. I tried to get Nick to sit down a few times and do a track-by-track accounting of all the songs he recorded with Megadeth and a tour-by-tour diary of shows, but he was difficult to pin down.

Nick always lived his life in the moment, rarely comfortable looking too far into the past and mostly unwilling to compromise his enjoyment by projecting too far into the future. Those things might have compromised the pleasure he got out of life and laughter—and he loved to laugh. He loved setting people up with outrageous statements and questions, if only to get a reaction and make people laugh. His love of all-things alien and conspiratorial... I could never tell what he truly believed and what he said just to get a rise out of me. Nick played mischief as if it were another instrument.

I called him up once in mock frustration, which I'm certain he loved. "Nick! What are you trying to do to me!?"

He'd done an interview on a radio show about this book, and he told the host, former Megadeth alumni Jeff Young, "I'll tell you this: inside the book, as you open the first cover page, there's an encrypted message in the writing and throughout the book itself that you're going to be able to read from beginning to end. Whoever is first to find what the message is will be able to come to the next level of the reading. But you'll have to figure out the code in there and where it shows up in the book. There's certain little clues inside that will grab your attention and you'll go, 'Hey, that's weird, I wonder why that's there on that page...' It's not something that's totally insane, but it's something that people are going to have to figure out, to find the real answer of what's happening, and the shocking deep message that I really have for everyone out there. The book will reveal itself in different ways, depending on how you interact with it."

It's not something that Nick had mentioned to me before going on the air. And after, I could almost see his grin over the phone, "Cool, eh? We can do that, right, Jeff?"

That's Nick. Nothing can't be done—or at least attempted—exhaustively. Is there an encrypted message throughout the book, leading to a "shocking deep message" from Nick?

You tell me.

Sure, his day-gig of "hitting things with sticks," as he calls it, is enormously cool to hear about. But there's a lot more to Nick's story than him playing in some band. He's very funny and wise, as you're about to discover. The son of famed jazz saxophonist Don Menza, Nick was blessed at birth, it seems, with an encyclopedic knowledge of music. He's humble, extremely kind, and generous. He's also a great cook (I gamble that comes from his wonderful mother. And, his father as well, as Don's sausage-and-pepper recipe would heartily suggest).

Amid the riches of traits and genuinely admirable quirks that constitute the résumé of Nick Menza—great conspiracy theorist, alien enthusiast, expert woodworker, outta-this-world artist, lover of comics and cartoons and all-things funny, animated or not—and one of the fiercest percussionists ever, this list could be a lengthy account in itself.

But I'd rather let Nick himself, and those who knew and loved him, fill in the blanks. As Nick's now distant drums still roll, let his final show begin.

Cape Cod,
July 1, 2018

INTRODUCTION

When the doctors told me the growth they'd removed from my knee was benign, I was so relieved I didn't think I had a worry in the world. I was stoked to be getting back on the Ozzfest 1998 tour, drumming for Megadeth, which I had been forced to take a break from for the procedure. When Dave Mustaine called me just two days after the surgery, I was expecting great news.

"Hey," he said. "We're going to let you go."

"Where? Disneyland? Don't fuck around dude. Now is not the time."

"I don't think you're hearing me clearly," he said.

That was it. My decade-long run with one of heavy metal's premiere bands at the height of its career was done. When it all came crashing down—when the drums stopped—it was bad. But I've survived; come out the other side with a renewed sense of purpose and heightened spirituality, and a profound desire to tell my truth with the sincere hope it has some positive effect or even inspires people, whether they know the public side of my story or not. I never thought I was interesting enough for a book, but my buddy J. Marshall (Jeff) Craig just came to me one day and said:

"Dude, let's write a book."

"About what?" I asked. "A bunch of lies, drugs, and sex on the road?"

He goes, "No, no, no. Your life, your story. People want to hear your end of the story."

"That's boring, dude. How boring for them."

But here we are. Jeff was right. Fans often ask me if I wish Dave had never fired me from the band. It took a while to realize that the answer's no. I sure didn't like how he did it, but Dave must have fired me a dozen times before. I don't know how many times I quit, but we always worked it out. Except for the last time. And there were a few "last times"; each one I was honestly hoping for, as were the fans.

We tried a reunion in 2004 that blew up almost immediately. Our last attempt, in late 2015, was promising, but Dave again lobbed an ego-grenade into the room. I had my time with Dave, and it was great. I don't make it a point to bash my former band members and diminish the memories of our great times together, but I'm not going to lie to you and hide the truth either.

I have great plans in my future. I will chart my own way and not rely on any shining reunion that I'm being treated like shit for. A chance to celebrate the great moments of the past together with our fans seemed real this time, but that doesn't appear to be in the cards. Like I have said in the past, I don't rule out rejoining Megadeth, and the opportunity would be totally cool. Even with what last went down with Dave, I'm open to whatever could possibly happen. That's up to him.

As frustrating as he can be, as bullheaded and sometimes childish, he's also a brother. We spent a lot of time together, during which I saw the great things about Dave and what a wonderful man he can be. Again, I wasn't happy about the way he fired me, over the telephone, but back then I ended up with a sense of relief and was overcome with a sense of freedom that I didn't have with Megadeth. It's like I forgot that music was fun—it's supposed to be done for the joy of it and not for getting paid and all the politics and crap that goes with it. It's like I forgot why I started playing music.

Yeah, dude, he gave me a cool gig. It's what I did, and drumming is what I do. But it's not who I am, and not who I want to be. I sure don't miss all the heavy travel and being away from home and, especially these days, all the hassle with immigration.

I've never said to myself, "I've made it; I've done it." I'm still waiting for that moment! No matter what scale you're at, you're always striving to get further and to get better.

At least I think you should be. I am.

The authors.

Looking back, I realize that Dave and I had been disagreeing on things for years. He was unhappy with the way things were going, and I was pretty unhappy and not doing anything to make the situation better. We were making less money, selling fewer records; doing smaller shows.

In the years since, Dave and I have talked, and we're cool when he's not being a dick with money.

He's a great teacher. I learned a lot from him, songwriting-wise—what to do, what not to do, how I'm going to do things differently for my band and the guys that I work with.

I'm proud of the ten years with those guys. It was a great experience, and I did some great work musically. There were a lot of fun times amidst the not-so-fun times.

What I do remember, I may not remember perfectly. I probably have some of the dates fucked up or have convinced myself something happened in Texas rather than Arizona. I never kept a diary, and, honestly, when we were out playing sometimes ten shows in a row with only one day's break, for weeks that turned into months—a lot of it's a haze.

Believe me, I've wracked my brain and gone through all the tour booklets I can still find tucked away in boxes at my house. I've looked at videos and photos and everything, and it's easy to remember the feeling I had at certain shows; but I can't remember the specifics, for the most part. It's like asking me if I can see my boys growing up and getting bigger right in front of my eyes every day. I can't—but when I look at birthday or Christmas photos every few years, it's like, "Dude! How did that happen?"

Same as when I look back. The sounds, smells, and tastes come back (which is sometimes alarming, let me tell you), but I don't remember too many of the really fine details.

What I do remember, however, is because of you, the fans. Thanks for listening. You guys are what's made it all worthwhile.

Nick Menza

Disintegrator Studios,
Studio City,
April 29, 2016

A HEAVY DRUMMER'S LIGHTER SIDE

(From a 2016 interview)

Q: *What would your ultimate Megadeth line-up look like?*

NICK: *Ten-foot tall aliens.*

Q: *Musically, where do you think Megadeth should venture? There's no debate that when you were in the band, Megadeth was a fiercer power, and sales prove it.*

NICK: *Outside the universe. That's because we were still selling records then. Now bands can't because of the interweb so....*

Q: *As all Mega-metal bands age in this digital age, what is the answer to make both band and fans happy?*

NICK: *Cold beer and air conditioning.*

Q: *Name three things that satisfy you as a musician, keeping the Megadeth formula in mind.*

NICK: *Sushi, pasta, tacos.*

Q: *What do you think fans want?*

NICK: *To come over to my house and hang out.*

Q: *When was the last time you seriously spoke with Dave about future collaborations?*

NICK: *Fourteen years ago.*

Q: *Who would you like to see on guitar for a full-on Rust In Peace reunion?*

NICK: *Randy Rhoads. That would be epic.*

(Nick to his manager, Rob Bolger: "Whoever wrote these questions is smoking shit without a screen.")

CHAPTER ONE

"JUST A REGULAR GIG"

I'd splashed coke all over my hands.

They were good and sticky, and I was ready to fucking tear up the place with Megadeth in front of a few hundred thousand crazy people. Coke... Coca-Cola...what the hell do you think I was doing? Sticky, sugary soda is the best way I've found to keep my drum sticks from slipping out of my sweaty hands. I'd heard about it from some pals who played professional football. And this was "Rock In Rio 2": something like two hundred thousand screaming people in one hundred degree heat and 100 percent humidity.

Getting my hands sticky had become part of my pre-show routine, and it paid off this night. We did our individual and group pre-show stuff, which always ended in a prayer with just the four members of Megadeth, holding (sticky) hands: "May the gift God has given you flow freely through you without any interference whatsoever."

Don't be surprised. The two Daves (Mustaine and Ellefson, who's called Junior to differentiate between them), Marty Friedman and I took it *very seriously* when we stepped up to play for you, no matter how it might have turned out.

In Rio that night, we were on fire. Our intro-tape started. Jello Biafra's "Message From Our Sponsor" over some Black Sabbath:

We interrupt this program with a special bulletin...
Remain calm, do not panic...

The last line of Biafra's piece was my cue to come on, alone, stand up on my drum riser, point to the audience, make a cross out of my sticks, and wind 'em up even more than they already were.

I'd mouth the words "House payment!" and sit down as the show began. No kidding. I'd thank the crowd, in my own stealthy way, for making my house payment. Believe me, it was with the greatest respect: an endearment. Like, "Let's get busy! I love you guys! Thank you for loving us!" I got asked about it only once, by someone from the T.J. Martell Foundation, the music industry's largest charity, funding innovative medical research focused on finding cures for leukemia, cancer, and AIDS. The foundation sources and supports early-stage research projects aimed at developing more effective clinical treatments for patients that otherwise might not be funded, which is huge. I can't think of a better cause to support. I got *so* nailed by one of these great kids, who could read lips. After a show in Southern California, one of the foundation representatives came up to me and asked, "Why do you come out and say, 'House payment?'"

Mustaine overheard and yelled out, "Ha! Busted, fucker!"

I rarely get nervous before a show, but that night in Rio was different.

By 1991, I'd been the drummer for Megadeth for three years, and I'd already seen it all. Well, except for a crowd that seemed to go on forever at a festival so huge it defied comprehension. I mean, just that single day, Wednesday, January 23, 1991, the crowd at the Maracanã Stadium was getting to hear Sepultra, Lobão, Megadeth, Queensrÿche, Judas Priest, and Guns N' Roses. Think of it—one day in Brazil with the craziest fans in the world. Truly, South American crowds are rad. They are the best, wildest crowds in the world. Over the years, when we'd play Buenos Aires we'd have to do four or five nights in a row just to satisfy the fans.

As incredible as such festivals can be and as exciting as it is to see so many people in an audience, the truth is that the sound generally isn't that good, and often the bands can't hear themselves on stage. I've always preferred smaller venues, whether I'm playing or watching one of my own favorite artists. They're more intimate and they sound better. Some of the coolest Megadeth gigs I did were surprise shows in clubs. On many of our tours, we quietly rented equipment or just used some house band's gear and hit a club as Vic & the Rattleheads. People would figure it out pretty quickly once we got there and started playing and the clubs would fill up. They were the most fun, close, and personal gigs. It's a different monster up there on the big stage, playing arenas—more theatrical, still playing the same shows, the same songs, but it doesn't sound as good unless there are a lot of people there to absorb the sound.

Here's one of the coolest things Mustaine ever told me: "I need you to know your shit. Play all the way through without anyone else playing. If you don't know your parts from beginning to end, by yourself, without hearing anyone else, then you don't really know the songs. I need you to know the songs." That was awesome. I knew the songs. I prided myself on knowing all my parts and knowing everything. Sure, I made mistakes—everybody does. Sometimes shit happens, with equipment, the weather, or you just get mental blocks like, "Oh no, coming up to that part again!" So, you cringe and play harder. I'd always know by the first song when we'd kick into a double-bass part whether I was going to have a good night or a challenging night, based on how easy it was for me to play that part. In "Wake Up Dead" there's a double-bass part in the middle section where we'd bust into this fucking locomotive beat that's just long enough before you start to seize up and then you're like, "Fuck I'm glad that's over with!"

Rio was probably the greatest lesson I ever learned about how crappy things can sound on stage at such huge venues. We had this sound guy named Gungy who was legendary. He had worked with all the greats, including Sabbath and Deep Purple. He was a monster in every great sense. He was about seven feet tall, with a Scottish accent and temper to match.

"My job is to take down a piece of the ceiling wherever you play," he once told me. And he sure tried. He did the strangest shit. Before sound-check, if we had one, he'd tune the PA to Nina Cherry or some weird vocal crap. I'd come up and ask him, "Dude, how can you do that? That's fuckin' *heinous*! What are you doing that for?"

"I need to hear if the speakers are blown," he said. "If I'm playing metal through there, I'm not gonna hear if they're crackin' or fuckin' fried. I need to hear if the horns are blown and I can't hear that with shredding guitars. Everything sounds blown. I need to make sure it's all dialed in."

He knew his shit. And he assured me that "No matter what you hear on stage, just know it's going to be dialed in out in the house. I'm going to see to it."

In Rio de Janeiro, he was right as always. We couldn't hear a thing on stage, ourselves or each other, but Megadeth rocked. That night, in front of a nuts crowd that faded into the horizon, none of us—no member of Supultera, Lobão, Megadeth, Queensrÿche, Judas Priest, or Guns N' Roses—was leaving anything to chance.

The four of us fucked around at the pool in the afternoon drinking whacky concoctions out of coconuts. We did some press and had some private time alone, took naps, worked out, had a little something to eat, watched some other bands, and scoped the massive crowd.

"It's just a regular gig," one of our tour staff said to me, trying to be helpful. Fuck that. No, it wasn't a regular gig.

Not long before we took the stage, Mustaine came to me, Junior, and Marty and told us that we had been given forty-five minutes, *maybe* fifty minutes, to play. And he wanted to get every song in our blistering two-hour set out there. No cuts.

"We're gonna play fast," he said.

"How fast?" I asked.

"I'm not cutting anything. *Fast.* I'll keep up."

Tell that to a drummer? Dude, you better mean it. And don't fade on me. When I see footage of that show now, it's almost comical. We were on fire. It was peak energy, and we slayed.

Before we stepped on stage, however, the whole thing was a mind fuck for me.

Rio was the climax of a whirlwind two years that started with Dave hiring me to take over the drum throne.

I am always a little surprised I ended up in Megadeth. That's the last band I would have suspected I'd be in, at least when I was starting out. I was shooting for other kinds of music (always rock 'n' roll, though) and skipping around L.A. bands. To be perfectly honest I really wasn't that into Megadeth when I first heard them. I liked a couple of their songs on *Peace Sells* but I can't say that I was a real fan before I met anyone in the organization or became their drum tech. I am as fierce as the next guy, but I actually always thought the name Megadeth was kind of limiting. Let's face it: it's just not universally acceptable. Hold your seat, but "Metallica" beat us in only two areas—record sales and cool name. You want to be massively huge. You want to be a household name and commercially listenable to all, but for some people, when they hear "Megadeth," it's like, "How nice for you. You totally worship the devil."

I started with the band a couple of years before I was in the band. First, I was officially the drum tech, but unofficially ended up being stage manager, truck driver, and guitar tuner. There was another dude who was supposed to be helping but he was totally blowing it so I was basically on my own. I finally went to the tour manager and said, "Dude, this is not happening. We gotta get some other guys in here. I can't tune the guitars and set up the drums and drive the truck and do all this shit myself. It's impossible. How much am I getting paid? Five hundred dollars a week? No. Not happening." But I kept doing it. Tuning those guitars for Mustaine, Junior, and Jeff Young, handing them over and then standing there at the side of the stage, waiting for the first chords. I'd be, "Whew! They're in tune!" That's stressful, man. They're always looking at you, asking, "Dude, where's my guitar, did you change the strings? Did you tune it?"

I learned to cut nuts for a guitar almost magically when Dave broke one while playing a club in Tacoma, Washington. I placed a match tip under the string and he went back out. That worked for the rest of the show. The next day I cut a less-makeshift one out of a piece of plastic from a comb, grooved it with a saw, and threw it on.

"Is that a graphite nut?" he asked.

"Sure, dude."

I learned how to do a lot of things right on the spot. I teched for them for about two years before friends began to ask out loud what I was thinking, that I was wasting my time and letting real drumming opportunities pass me by. But what few knew was that every day on the road, I'd often set up Chuck's kit twice. The first time I'd to it for me in some out-of-the-way place in the venue, where I could practice for hours, and then a second time when I set his gear up on stage for the show. I was working my ass off for very little money, but I was traveling the world and getting paid to practice for four to six hours a day sometimes. That was not wasting my time. But I was getting bored. I was thinking of telling Mustaine that I was going to move on when, one night at the Hammersmith Odeon in London, Chuck didn't show up. I ended up getting on the drums at the soundcheck and Dave asked, "What songs do you know?"

"All of 'em," I said.

He didn't believe me.

"Do you know this one?" He started playing "Holy Wars," which he still hadn't finished writing and certainly hadn't recorded yet.

I nailed it.

Dave came up to me, smiled, and shook my hand but didn't say anything.

"What?" I asked.

"You know what."

"No," I said, "I don't know what. If Chuck doesn't show up, I can do the show?"

"Yeah, I know," Dave said. "We'll talk later."

Chuck finally appeared and didn't fuck up that night, or for a short while after. I finally got bored with being the tech and standby drummer, sitting in the wings waiting for him to get fired. Finally, I quit and went home. I wanted to *play*, dude. Dave had never told me this before he hired me, but he said in interviews later that he had me around not just because I was a great drum tech, but because he knew I could cut it if Chuck really blew it and a show was in jeopardy. "Nick was there as a drummer waiting for Chuck to fuck up," he said to one interviewer. If he'd told me that flat out in the beginning, I still don't know that I would have hung in. But it didn't matter. I wasn't home long—a month or so, I think. The phone rang one night, and I thought it was one of my friends messing with me when he said he was Mustaine. I told him to fuck off and hung up. The phone rang again. This time it clearly wasn't a prank. It was Ron Laffitte, Megadeth's manager.

"Dude," he said, "Dave Mustaine's only going to call you once and offer you the job!"

"That was Mustaine? No way!"

I called Dave back, and he said, "You're the guy. Let's do this."

Those are words I'd been waiting to hear since I picked up sticks.

I was pumped, so excited about the future, but it was not to be an easy road. Through the summer and fall, we jammed and rehearsed sporadically. Mustaine was battling his self-destructive ways, and Junior's only real priority was getting himself off alcohol and heroin for the final time. He was doing really well. Mustaine, not so much.

We headed into the studio for the first, and only time, as a trio. We weren't able to get into Sound City because it was booked, as usual, and to be honest we weren't sure when we were going into the studio to get into the next record. Our first effort won't go down as a particularly stellar moment as we recorded a cover of Alice Cooper's "No More Mister Nice Guy" for the 1989 Wes Craven horror film *Shocker*. Dave's vocal is cool; very aggressive as usual. It was fun to do, of course, but Junior and I never really knew what kind of shape we were going to find Dave in day to day. At that time, frankly, seeing what Dave was doing to himself and the band was reinforcement to not do drugs.

We all cringed at the news when Dave got busted for impaired driving and his tox screen revealed something like ten prescriptions and illegal drugs in his system. For the first of many times, he was shipped off to rehab before Megadeth could get off the ground.

Early into 1990, the first order of business was to find a guitarist to fill Jeff Young's shoes. We had a rad rehearsal hall in the Valley, and Dave made I don't know how many calls. Dimebag Darrell of Pantera was offered the gig over the phone, but he wouldn't join the band without his brother Vinnie coming along to play drums. (I got to become very good friends with Darrell and Vinnie, two absolutely awesome guys. Darrell's on-stage murder was, for me, pretty much the worst musical memory since the killing of John Lennon.) Criss Olivia was offered the job and, I heard, was seriously considering the move, but graciously declined the offer and continued with his brother and Savatage. Lee Altus of Heathen and Eric Meyer of Dark Angel fame came through, and Jeff Waters of Annihilator was offered the gig, too. Slash had been hanging out jamming and partying. He loved not having to deal with Axl. Imagine that. I almost felt sorry for the nearly constant stream of poor bastards that flowed in, and then quickly out, of the doors, trying to land their dream gig of playing lead for Megadeth. And I felt sorry for myself! I was the henchman who had to tell them, "Thanks for coming in. Good luck." Many of them didn't stay for the length of a single song. Seriously, it sucked. The two Daves would turn their wirelesses off without saying a word and walk out of the room. The wannabe guitar player would be standing there looking at me like, "What's up?"

One week alone, more than fifty guys tripped through. Most of them were bozos, playing over Dave's leads and playing solos where there shouldn't have been solos. We videotaped all of them and would get together and laugh our asses off at some of these dudes. Some knuckleheads didn't have a professional concept about really learning the songs, but others were nice cats in a field of some serious fucking competition. No one rose to the surface that fit us perfectly and came without conditions. As it turned out, Mustaine gave a second shot to one of his earlier rejects, Marty Friedman of Cacophony. Dave hated Marty's Jewish name and his multicolored hair, his cheap Carvin guitar and Carvin amp; even his jeans. "Honestly, I love the little guy," Mustaine said once, "but he looked like a poser to me, because his hair was two different colors." He wasn't what Dave was "looking" for. But Dave knew what he heard, and Marty was what we were "listening" for. So, Marty was enrolled in what Dave called "Rock School 101."

"He was tattered, he had crap gear, his blue jeans were ripped up, he had cheesy cheap high-tops on, and he looked like he needed his hair cut," Dave said later in interviews. "He looked like a typical starving Hollywood guitar student/guitar teacher. So, we put him through the ringer, got rid of his crap; got him back in line with playing Jackson guitars. We made sure that he had money to move to a real apartment. Got him a car. Made him get his personal hygiene in touch with where he is now. He got his hair all one color. And after a week, we said, 'Well, I've got some bad news for you, dude, you're in the band.'"

In March, Junior marked what would become his "birthday" sobriety date. Marty was aboard and Dave and Junior were both healthy. Thankfully, we didn't just go into the studio and write a new record. Instead, we worked through the spring and summer getting to know each other musically, and getting introduced to that mysterious, magical fifth member of the group—the monster that appeared out of the heavy metal ether only when the two Daves, Marty and I were *on*. Maybe that's the real Vic Rattlehead.

We worked relentlessly through the next year, more than one thousand rehearsals by my count, to get ourselves, and our first songs, in shape. When we were ready that fall, we headed into Rumbo Recorders, the recording studio owned by Captain & Tennille, where there was a killer pedigree of rock 'n' roll history.

We were clean, sober, and ruthless.

Mustaine brought in Mike Clink, who in turn brought engineer Micajah Ryan and producer Dave Jerden aboard to help out, since Clink was also working with Guns N' Roses in another room at the studio. The rest of us were stoked, since Ryan is a monster, and Jerden was so well known for being at the helm of Alice in Chains' *Facelift, Sap,* and *Dirt,* along with The Offspring's *Americana,* Red Hot Chili Peppers' *Mother's Milk*—not to mention Zappa, the Stones, Jane's Addiction, and Anthrax. The dude has a résumé.

Mustaine fired Jerden first thing.

"I think there's too many guys named Dave around here," I recall him saying. "We're gonna get rid of one of them."

Bye-bye, Mr. Jerden.

There was a seriously happy ending, however, since that is when the incredible Max Norman first came in to help us be everything we could be in the studio. Max helped Mustaine and Ryan finish the record, which we ended up calling *Rust In Peace.* And, of course, Max was there to help steer us on our next outing with *Countdown To Extinction* which, together, are hands down the best records Megadeth ever made and ever will make—whether Marty and I are in the band or not. I don't think many fans will disagree. We were recording live, *not* to a click track. We were recording analog, and we weren't trying to be commercial—not trying to *be* anything. We were making *our* music, and that's it.

The album and title track got their name from Mustaine having seen a bumper sticker that said, "May your nuclear weapons rust in peace."

Pretty much the theme that Dave's always been into: nukes and annihilation and all that. Hell, if you don't know, he got the name for the band when he was on a bus back to California after Metallica fired him. He was reading a pamphlet about nuclear weapons and their "megadeath" casualties. The tune "Holy Wars" came out of Dave's ignorant comment in Northern Ireland the year before, when he drunkenly incited the Protestants and Catholics in the audience to riot by dedicating a song to the "conflict," which he didn't realize meant the IRA. At the time they were conducting terrorist attacks in the North and in England.

The tune "Hangar 18," which gave us our first radio-friendly hit, was based on my lyrics about the aliens from the Roswell crash site, which had been sent by truck to an Air Force hangar (#18!) in Ohio, before finally being moved back to Area 51, where they are today, working in the mess hall. The music was from a song sketch Dave had been working on when he'd been fired from Metallica. ("That must have really sucked to have been fired from the band he loved," I thought. This was before I knew what it was like.)

11

Looking back, "Hangar 18" was the first sign that Dave and I were going to have a fairly tumultuous creative relationship. He never knew when to take me seriously and when not to, and I have never really understood people who take everything so seriously. Life's too short to not have fun; do what you want, and make as much magic as you can. Dave was totally not into UFOs and aliens, but he liked the lyrics I wrote. Thereafter, it just became fun to tease him about extraterrestrial shit every chance I got. One time, I told him that Jesus had to have been born of higher beings from another dimension, which would explain his virgin birth. It was artificial insemination. He wasn't into that and took offense. Seriously, I didn't mean to offend him. I just think everything we can't explain is worth thinking about, to acknowledge the wonder of it all. Relax. It's a great tune!

We were a machine going into Rumbo to record, and we were unstoppable once we were in there. I did all my drum tracks in a little over a week, and Marty recorded the best solo to ever be laid down on a heavy metal song in "Tornado of Souls."

In the many years since, it's sad that Dave can't back off when the spotlight dims just the smallest amount on him. He has claimed that he wrote all of Marty's parts by humming them. What a fucking birdbrain. Nobody on this—or any other planet—could have done what Marty did. He also claims he "wrote" all my drum parts for that matter. Nice try, dude. You've been able to hire competent imitators of both of us and that's about it. We showed the world, in two albums, what the four of us could do when unencumbered by drugs and booze, and able to keep self-centered egos from getting in our way. None of us has ever come close again, but that's ok. You can't get that close to the sun and not expect to burn up.

When *Rust In Peace* was released, it sold more than a million copies out of the gate in the U.S. and received Grammy nominations in 1991 and 1992 for Best Metal Performance. My first album with Megadeth is either the best or the second-best depending on which fans you ask. We got five Grammy nominations when I was in the band, which was something I never thought I'd experience. A win would have been nice, but it was pretty cool every year getting the nod.

With Mom and Gumby.

By the time those thousand rehearsals and *Rust In Peace* were done, my first gig with the band was in Riverside, California on September 10, 1990. It was our premiere of "Holy Wars" and "Hangar 18," the first song I wrote with Dave, in a set that included "Rattlehead," "In My Darkest Hour," "Good Mourning/Black Friday," "Liar," and "Anarchy in the U.K." I was so well rehearsed, but that's the way it's supposed to be. The way it had to be. I was nervous as fuck. I was so nervous that I was exhausted the night before from not sleeping, and when I finally did fall asleep, I was such a zombie that I got up in the middle of the night to take a piss, forgot where I was, whacked my foot into the wall getting out of bed and pretty much freaked out. The next day I made the mistake of telling everyone what had happened and they never, for the next ten years, let me forget about being the "rock-star drummer who is afraid of the dark." Fuckers.

The guys in Metallica were at that show. I was jazzed that they'd come and thought it was cool that they were there out of respect, not to see Mustaine fuck up and prove them right for having fired his ass all those years before. But right after we were done, Dave said, "Let's get in the car and bail." I asked why we didn't hang and Dave was like, "Fuck those guys. I'm going to put you through Rock School," he said. "Once you graduate, you're going to know how to handle situations like this."

I'd been the drum tech for a couple of years, and though we'd now been working for a year solid on the new lineup, I admit I was still a novice about being in the band. And, when it came to "Rock School," Mustaine was always right. That first gig was a thousand rehearsals, but I learned in just ninety short minutes everything *not* to do. Everything's not going to be perfect every time you play. And every time you go out, you have to rely on your knowledge and experience as well as your talent. You learn quickly how to pace yourself, and how to do all the things you couldn't do at the beginning of rehearsals or the start of the tour.

Less than a month after *Rust In Peace* hit the streets, so did we, joining Slayer, Suicidal Tendencies, and Testament for the European Clash of the Titans Tour. We were unstoppable. The two Daves were on fire, Marty was the best in the world, and I was learning the lessons of a lifetime, how to pace myself (crucial for playing drums in Megadeth!) and learning things that up until then I hadn't been able to do. That Megadeth lineup was truly great, unless we were having a shitty night, which was pretty rare on our first two tours. There are bands that certainly got bigger than us and sold more records, but nobody could fucking touch us live. Nobody.

My years in the band allowed me to pretty much master the drums. I can play any type of music. I'll get up and play with anyone, anytime, whether I know the songs or not; music and math are the two universal languages. You get up there, sit down and listen, and if you hear the music you'll know what to play. It's like having a conversation. I used to be intimidated by certain types of music (intricate, precise stuff like jazz), but once I started playing metal, which is the most physically strenuous and demanding music to play, any music was easy for me. It just became about keeping my head clear and "doing the math" with my heart and soul.

We were riding high. The next month we were added as the opening act on Judas Priest's Painkiller Tour, climaxing with that landmark performance in January 1991 at Rock In Rio 2.

From there, we kept blazing, kicking off the Clash of the Titans Tour in the U.S. in May of '91 with Slayer, Anthrax, and Alice in Chains. We did the first of our shows as Vic & the Rattleheads in San Francisco, which was a blast. I loved those hit-and-run club gigs. So intimate, so ear-bleeding. The fans went nuts. In July, our "Go to Hell" track was featured on the *Bill & Ted's Bogus Journey* soundtrack. Shortly after, "Breakpoint" was featured on the *Super Mario Bros.* soundtrack. That summer, we released our first home video, *Rusted Pieces*, which contained six music videos as well as a video interview with the four of us. I always liked the idea of doing videos and documenting what we were doing in the studio, but they never turned out the way they should have. They could all have been a lot more creative, instead of the usual lame heavy metal stuff. They were an afterthought, when nothing we do for the fans should be an afterthought.

Megadeth was soaring in the age of alt-rock, which was crushing everything else in its path. In the fall of 1991, we took a month off the road to begin writing the next record and start stepping up our rehearsals. After the Christmas break with our families, we returned to the studio on January 6, 1992, this time at Enterprise Studio in Burbank. By April 28, *Countdown To Extinction* was born. Musically, I think it's the most accomplished record we made. *RIP* sounds a lot better because we were all clean and sober and recorded live, without a click track—the way I favor recording—but I'm in the minority. Max was back, this time as producer, and Mustaine let him be key to our musical makeover, pushing for shorter, less complicated, and more radio-friendly songs, though just as heavy, if not heavier, than ever before. We were in the studio for four months writing and recording, unlike *RIP*, which was already written when we went into the studio. This was the first of our records to include writing contributions from every member, not just Mustaine and Junior. I wrote the lyrics for "Countdown to Extinction" and recommended that it be the title track.

At Enterprise Studio with Max Norman and RIP plaques.

It came out in the summer of 1992 and was an instant hit, debuting in the No. 2 spot on *Billboard*. For the first time we hit two million in sales. "Symphony of Destruction," "Foreclosure of a Dream," and "Sweating Bullets" were the hits that made us double platinum out of the gate. We didn't win (again) but it was the second time a record I played on earned a Grammy nomination. And the title track has the distinction of being the only metal song to win the "Doris Day Music Award," presented by the Humane Society for its narrative on species destruction. That was pretty cool. Not sure I'll ever be on a record that gets that award again, but never say never, right?

A world tour in support of the record was launched in December 1992, with Pantera and Suicidal Tendencies supporting. The tour included a North American leg in January 1993 with opening act Stone Temple Pilots, which I was pumped about. STP was an awesome band

and I, for one, just had this feeling that they were probably going to blow right past us in record sales and popularity (which they did). However, they joined the long list of bands that couldn't touch us live. When we weren't fucked up on drugs, that is. By this time, Mustaine was back into the booze and drugs in the only way he knew how—full on.

Scott Weiland was an elusive and quiet dude, really intense and in his own head. He, too, was already walking the line with drugs and alcohol. Like Dave, he was a sweet, tortured guy whose problems swept up everybody around him. Scott and I clicked from the start, but I'm not sure how close he ever really got to anyone.

I don't know that Scott ever made it much past treading water with sobriety, which sucks, because he was an enormous talent and, truly, the sweetest dude when he was straight. His death in 2015 didn't come as a shock to me, I am sad to say. I know he really tried to get his life together and keep it there, despite not being able to get more than a few months clean at any one time. That sucked. Mustaine always had trouble helping himself, but he was right there for Scott, along with Duff, Slash, and a long list of Scott's family, friends, and bandmates. You can throw the lifelines, but you can't force someone to hold on.

For the short time we were out with STP, Scott refused to do soundchecks, so I'd go out and sing Zeppelin tunes with the band. It was a blast. It would be cool to hear some of those tapes if they exist. Stone Temple Pilots is one of my favorite bands of the day.

The tour, which was full of the promises of Japan and then Australia, was short-lived. We were about a month out when Mustaine swallowed a whole bottle of Valium after a show in Oregon ended in a riot. He overdosed on our bus on the way back to the hotel and ended up clinically dead in an ER. Suicide attempt, not a suicide attempt, just a monumental near-fatal fuckup...does it really matter? He survived, which was the only truly important thing.

The whole tour, including a month's dates scheduled in Japan, was cancelled as he was shipped off to rehab again, and the rest of the band and crew scattered in various directions home. Had he not overdosed that night, we might have kept on for a time, with him in an ever-escalating and perilous state that probably would have ended with him dying somewhere on the road. So, no matter how shitty and frustrating things ever became, the worst, at least, never happened. Still, I have wondered what might have come of those first Japanese shows.

Of all the places in the world, my two favorites were South America, for the insane crowds, and Japan, for the crews. Life on the road is exciting, of course, for the first few trips around the world. But no matter who you are, when the weeks turn into months of not seeing your family, and the hotel rooms, buses, and airplanes become a blur of luggage, you start to forget where you are and where you're going. You're fucking lost if you don't have your tour book with you. When you start to recognize the same hotel room in Paris or Rome, it's anticlimactic. At least it was for me. But Japan was a breeze.

Dave Ellefson:
As much as we broke into it in 1991 with Rock in Rio, South America became a home away from home for us. A lot of other markets were trendy and would come and go, the popularity always subject to a lot of other things, but South America was one market that was truly ours and still is. I have great memories of going to Argentina with Nick and playing five nights in Buenos Aires, then getting into the van after the show while kids were jumping on top and pounding on the windows, and feeling like they were going to smash through. It was just the thin glass of the windows that protected them from getting to us. Your life is literally on the line; at least that's what it felt like. Those are experiences that you have with your brothers that I got to have with Nick. When you go through those, it bonds you in a way that's almost thicker than blood. When you live for your craft, and almost die for it, it creates a brotherhood that lives on forever. I'm really glad I got to have those experiences and those moments with my brother Nick.

The people are amazing and those shows in Japan were the easiest ever—for us and for our road crews. The crowds are the polar opposite of

South American crowds, which are like a full-blown riot on quiet nights. The Japanese crews are like surgeons. They show up early and watch your crew set up your gear the first night of the tour, taking meticulous photographs and notes of everything, and I mean everything. For the remainder of the shows in Japan, you show up at 7:00, there's no opening act, you're off stage by 9:00 and out on the town stuffing your face with sushi and hanging out.

The next night, the next city, you come up on stage and your shit is dialed in exactly like it was the night before. Nothing against the awesome crews we always had, but in Japan it's perfect: every piece of equipment, every dial and knob precise. Our crew could start the party early. All they had to worry about were our actual performance needs. The Japanese crews would tear down, load the trucks, drive to the next venue, and it would, again, be picture-perfect.

I wish to god that had been what happened on the tour with Stone Temple Pilots. We all do.

If Rock in Rio was the highlight, Overdose in Oregon was the low point. Things would never be as good again for any sustained period.

After about two months in treatment, Mustaine was cleaned up and we immediately went into a dingy little studio in Phoenix to record Dave's song "Angry Again" for the Schwarzenegger film *Last Action Hero*. The song earned us our fourth Grammy nomination.

When we were ready again for the road, we went as special guests at Metallica's Milton Keynes Bowl Festival, marking the first time Megadeth and Metallica had played the same stage in the decade since Metallica had fired Dave. We did a great club show as Vic & The Rattleheads at Nottingham's Rock City two days before, which was off the dial in more ways than

one. By this time, Dave was again out of control, and there was no pre-dicting whether a show was going to be fabulous or fucked up.

We joined Aerosmith in support of their massive Get A Grip Tour, which was exciting for us, opening for heroes of ours, but it all came to an embarrassing and shameful stop just seven shows in, when we were fired because of Dave (details to follow, I promise!).

Dave went back to rehab and the rest of us scattered. Junior started work with metal act Helstar and Marty got busy on another solo record.

After that latest twelve-step sojourn of Dave's, we went back into Enterprise in North Hollywood to record "99 Ways to Die" for *The Beavis and Butt-Head Experience*. It was a great take that almost didn't see the light of day when the tape machine mangled the master. Thankfully, it was salvaged, and got us yet another Grammy nomination. Later in that session we did a cover for a Black Sabbath tribute album. At first, we couldn't agree on what track to do. Mustaine launched into "Paranoid" and we all fell in. It rocked. That was a fun one.

Before we went in to do the next record, though, the band decided to release the EP *Hidden Treasures*, which was a masterful move. For all those early years, Megadeth was one of the go-to bands that every movie producer (well, the producers of certain kinds of movies) wanted for their soundtracks. It was cool recording some of our favorite metal covers to accommodate them. What sucked, though, was that there were a bunch of Megadeth songs that fans wanted which were only available in some movies that really blew. We compiled the tracks on *Hidden Treasures* so you wouldn't have to see all these bad movies or get their soundtracks to hear them.

When Dave was healthy again, he decided he didn't want to record in L.A. He, Junior, and Marty all lived in Phoenix at this point, so for the sixth record, my third with Megadeth, we congregated in Arizona. Dave brought Max Norman back again. At first, we went into Phase Four Studios, but it was a mess. There weren't really any viable alternatives, so Max suggested we buy a house and build our own studio where we could also all live together. It was divine fate that this didn't happen. I hate to think of what fresh horrors would have befallen us if it really came together and Megadeth had its very own summer of Nellcote (the French villa where the Stones so infamously lived and partied their way into hedonistic legend while writing and recording one of the greatest rock 'n' roll records ever: *Exile on Main St.*). The Stones were the pros, the kings of the stoned age when it came to living, loving, and licking up the finer things of rock 'n' roll mayhem.

Things had been great between us for a while, but rifts were beginning to show. Living together in a house and working 24/7? There isn't a house big enough in Phoenix for us to have done that without ending up as heinous stains on what would have been left of the walls and carpets. But the way it worked out was very cool. Instead of the house, Max found us a warehouse on the edge of town, which was awesome.

Dave Ellefson:

Countdown To Extinction was a big turning point for Megadeth in terms of the music, the pressure we put upon ourselves, the lifestyle changes, celebrity. Everything that came at us, from girls to drugs...suddenly everything we ever wanted was coming our way and it was frightening. It was the very thing that befell so many of our contemporaries. But it was a very interesting time: playing on MTV, traveling the world; the record coming out at number two on the Billboard chart. We were truly celebrated rock stars. That record was a stepping-stone to things that would follow. By the time we did Youthanasia in Arizona, Nick was the only one who didn't move because he is such a born-and-bred-in-the-valley boy. Making that record was so cool, because unlike all the pressures we went through since Countdown, suddenly we could buy a little time; create a little space. This organic feeling came over us where we were really working together as a group. It's always been one of my favorite periods creatively for Megadeth.

While construction was fast-tracked, overseen by Max and Dave, I got to spend lots of time out on the desert trails mountain biking. I'm not crazy about cameras being around all the time, but the decision was made to chronicle the making of the album, which came out as the documentary *Evolver: The Making of Youthanasia*. Looking back, it's a pretty cool snapshot of what was going on in the band at the time and just how good Megadeth was when we were all in a creative, positive space.

Donia Menza (Nick's sister):
When Nick made it into Megadeth, he hated photo shoots. He did not enjoy having his picture taken or having cameras around. When it came time for family photos and holidays, he would always complain. That's why most of his photos are so serious. Over time, he warmed up to it, especially when it was a meet-and-greet with fans. That's when the funny faces started to appear. Soon after, he would be so comfortable in front of the camera you could hardly keep him away from it. Then the short video clips started to appear and there was no stopping him. He found humor in the most uncomfortable circumstances.

We managed to deflate a lot of the posturing, at least on camera, and everybody got along and showed his best side. We did our songwriting and pre-production in Vintage Recorders in Phoenix before heading into the new studio, which was dubbed "Fat Planet in Hangar 18." Behind the scenes, of course, things were different. The band, crew, recording team, and management were all trying to keep Dave on track. We had our own versions of interventions with him, because so much was at stake every time we went into a studio and especially every time we went out on the road. We couldn't afford to have any more cancelled tours, either financially or critically. At some point, the promoters and the fans all say, "fuck you."

Dave was resistant and pissed, but none of that made it into the documentary.

We were never a band to rest on our laurels, and Dave's vision for the directions he wanted to go with serious lyrics always dictated the compass we'd use. He can be a dick, but there's nobody better at writing heavy metal songs than Dave Mustaine.

The title *Youthanasia*, is not a spelling mistake. I don't know what birdbrain started that lame rumor. Dave's a genius with lyrics and tackling pretty harsh social themes. He's always tended to think above the critics' heads. What other metal band has the balls to tackle the theme of international child exploitation? You know, kids being hung out to dry? It was a great concept, and the graphic cover even got us banned in Singapore. You know you're making a rad statement when you get banned somewhere.

This was the first time the band tuned down a half step. We didn't mess with tunings a whole lot, but I loved it when we did. While construction was going on at the warehouse, we assembled for two months at Vintage Recorders, which has a huge rock 'n' roll pedigree. Just before we got together, Marty and I had laid down some sketches at my place in North Hollywood, and we came up with the chorus part of "I Thought I Knew it All." It's a great *LOUD* track. "A Tout Le Monde" is about Dave's overdose in Oregon. It's the record's highlight. "The Killing Road" is obviously about life on tour. Sometimes touring can be a drag. I'll tell ya, it gets hard if I have a cold or something. If I am not feeling well, that is when the morale goes down. But, for the most part, this is really what I live for—having the opportunity to play in front of people. In every city that we go to, the hour and a half that I spend up on the stage pretty much outweighs all the crap that I have to deal with during the day in terms of traveling, hotels, and bad food. There are so many negatives throughout the day that the positive of being on stage and seeing the enjoyment of the fans causes you to forget about all that stuff. Of course, if you go for three, four, six, or eight months without even getting to go home, after you've done it for a few years, you burn out. I know, rock stars bitching about achieving their dreams but, dude, sometimes that thing about being careful for what you wish for....

We had fun in Phoenix, and the guys were right to want to record there. Being away from all that really helped us.

A lot of this record was written and recorded on the spot, showing off the sheer power of the band at the time. We all contributed. It was a lot of work and money to build a studio for one album.

I love recording live. I like having the pressure on me, because I'm the dude who only gets one crack at it. If I blow it, we have to go back and do it over or if I'm not happy with my take, or if Dave wasn't happy with it. Everyone else can nail his take, but if my part wasn't happening, the whole take was no good because of the way we were recording. You can go back and fix guitars or whatever, but it's a death knell to be punching in the master drum tracks.

I watched the documentary again recently, and it was cool to revisit. I don't like watching myself, but I stand by my comment that "Dave is so intense and has such a vision of what he wants to do. And it is, you know, Dave's dream, and fortunately, he's been kind enough to dream me in."

What nobody sees, and we never let the cameras record, of course, were the times that weren't so good between us. Dave had started drinking and using again, and rather than get a handle on his problems, roped us all in, so that we all had to participate in group therapy sessions and counseling. Watch the film and ask yourself why I'm out mountain biking so much.

It ended up being a long haul, taking us something like seven or eight months to record. Way too long for me to be away from home, even with breaks almost every weekend. The record's a lot more polished, focusing on stronger vocal melodies and more accessible, radio-friendly arrangements. MTV did a *Night of the Living Megadeth* broadcast, and the next day, when it was released, it went gold in Canada in just half an hour. It was our fastest record to reach platinum in the States. It brought us to a wider and stronger audience that came out for the tour over the next relentless year. We were out with Flotsam and Jetsam, Korn, Fear Factors, Alice, and Ozzy. The two years around *Youthanasia* and its tour became a blur. It was exhausting.

One of the highlights was our first-ever show in Tel Aviv. That was a trip. If we'd had cameras on the road, that would have been the experience to catch on film.

The tour wasn't fun, however. It was tense, from all aspects. Mustaine was struggling to stay clean, and insisted on the band and crew being straight as well. That was cool with everybody, except we again had to do group therapy and attend band AA meetings and do piss tests. Well, we were told to do piss tests. The rest of the band and the entire crew signed and pissed happily into plastic cups, while I was the sole holdout. Things got physical after a long flight to London. Mustaine confronted me, grabbed me by the throat, and threatened to kill me. Our security pulled him off. I should have pissed on his leg right then and there. I stood my ground. I never piss-tested for anyone. Ever.

But all this tension had the expected effect on us. The first sign that things, outwardly, were heading in a bad direction was Dave firing our manager, Ron Laffitte. Industry veteran Bud Prager was brought in. He was a fine man with a great résumé, but Bud was not the dude for Megadeth. Dave caused us the worst instability to date, without the management and talent behind the studio console that we needed.

What became *Cryptic Writings* was not our style and not a comfortable session. The band was coming under the control and direction of the people who had done Foreigner. What the fuck was *that* all about? I don't remember a lot of the tour that followed, since everyone was miserable. Even the fans were pretty miserable because we'd done a sucky pop record—at least by the standards of Megadeth.

In fact, I don't remember much from the whole time except for when doctors told me that my knee wasn't fucked up because of a strain or torn tendon or anything like that. Instead, I learned I had a tumor. As I look back, I think that was the beginning of the end for me and for the classic lineup of Megadeth, especially after Dave ditched Max, who I always regarded as our secret weapon in the studio, and brought in Mike Renault and Bud Prager.

Nirvana and the wave of grunge out of the Northwest was drowning the whole music world, and instead of getting tougher, louder, raunchier, and faster, Megadeth went the other way. What we were wearing and what our hair was like became more important than ever. But the shit that really got to me was that Prager tried to turn us into what he was most famous for: Foreigner. He changed what shoes we wore and what notes we played, and it sucked, dude. I don't know why Dave went along with it, except to say that, at the time, he was so out of it and had so lost control that he didn't know what he was doing, besides having a hard-on for a No. 1 record. That would have been cool if it had been a No. 1 Megadeth record.

"Trust" is a cool song, I admit, and I tried my best to make the thing fucking soar on the drums. But one or two tracks isn't a strong album. Not by the standards we'd set with our first outings. None of the rest of us had the power to stop the train we were on. The whole thing became miserable. The way we treated and related to each other was miserable. We did the record in Nashville with Prager's golden-boy producer Donn Huff, a pop producer who ended up ghostwriting a lot of the music and lyrics with Dave, revising the songwriting to "better reflect the sales and radio airplay environment of the rock arena," as we were told.

For years now, Dave has gone on and on about how clever we were with that record, that the band's commercial breakthrough came from the "fact that we're willing to study the marketplace and educate ourselves." Seriously, dude? Fuck me. It's this kind of shit that gave rise to punk bands and heavy metal in the first place.

Yes, Dave and David and Marty and Nick had our first and only No. 1 record with the track "Trust." Yes, we were getting more radio play than ever before. But it wasn't a Megadeth record the way *Rust In Peace* and *Countdown* were. Marty was clearly disillusioned with the direction Dave was taking us in—or letting us stumble into blindly, saying stuff like, "Maybe the future for us is to have no distortion." I was like, "Dude, you're in the wrong band."

We had a fucking seventy-year-old who knew nothing about metal managing us and cloth-eared engineers and producers wanting us to be Foreigner 2.0. The way I came to see it, the *band* was in the wrong band.

In interviews, I did my best to bullshit how I felt about it, saying things like, "Um...this is just another point in time for us," and, "This record is reminiscent of early Megadeth stuff. It's hungry and has a lot of fire on it." How about, "We're playing hard!" Yeah, lame, but that's all I could muster.

Just put *Cryptic Writings* on and give it a listen; you'll hear it right there in the tunes. It sucks. Well, as a Megadeth record, anyway, and that's what we were supposed to be making. It was the only artistic, critical, and commercial failure with me and Marty in the band, and there wasn't our usual excitement to go out and promote it for its own sake, though we knew that we wouldn't be playing much of it on the road. And we didn't. We played *Rust In Peace* and *Countdown* and *Hidden Treasures* and earlier tracks.

From the moment I was in the band, we were focused and aligned with what we wanted to do and how we wanted to do it. We were always the type of band that makes the music for ourselves first. I believe that is why our music has so much substance to it. It is real. It is reality. It is not like we are trying to contrive shit that we think people are going to like. Our attitude was always, "If people don't like it, that's okay because we do." We are the ones that get up there and play it every day. Everything about us, and *that* band, changed the second Dave and Prager and Huff decided that we should do a Metallica record rather than a Megadeth record.

Once the tour kicked off, we did our first acoustic performances ever, in South America, and again settled into one of our grueling world tours. By the following spring, I was starting to have trouble with one of my knees, which was sometimes seriously painful during and right after shows. We were scheduled to begin with Ozzfest '98 at the end of June. I had been trying to push through, and pushed myself too hard, figuring I could somehow do the summer tour, as we were snaking our way through the Southwest. But by June 9, it was too much. I despise having to go to doctors, but I had no choice because I knew that it was about to start causing me problems with my performances. I figured it was a strain or a torn tendon or some bullshit—I'd need some steroids, a tight tension-bandage wrap or something; maybe a few painkillers for after the shows.

Not so lucky.

The doctors told me I had a tumor.

Cancer? They didn't know and wouldn't be able to make a determination until they'd done a biopsy. I was a basket case, wondering whether it was cancer; whether I'd lose my leg, or worse.

I refused the biopsy. I told them to take the fucking thing out of me so that I wouldn't have to have one little pussy surgery and then go back in and have another if the tumor was malignant.

Still, I kept putting off the operation. One night on the bus something like two weeks in to the tour, Dave saw me slumped in a seat, near tears from the combination of the pain and the fear that not only my career, but my life, was in danger.

Dave was really kind, gentle, and loving as he sat with me. He told me straight out that I had to stop fucking around with it and get my knee looked after. The tour doctors said it would be about a three-week ordeal, at best, and then hopefully I'd be back playing before August was out.

Dave told me to not worry about it. I'd be fine and back on the throne in a few weeks. In the meantime, he said former Suicidal Tendencies drummer Jimmy DeGrasso would fill my shoes while I was out of the picture. Jimmy had worked with Dave on his solo MD45 project or whatever it was. Their history made Jimmy the obvious guy to fill in for a few shows. I just wanted to be back happenin' for the next record, the next tour.

"Dude, go handle that," Dave told me. "If it was me, I'd have it fuckin' taken out right now."

"Well I have to get a couple more tests taken," I said.

I kept putting it off, but I finally realized I couldn't make it through the tour. I didn't have a choice. I couldn't go on playing the way I was, physically or emotionally, since I was so twisted about how the doctors couldn't give me a straight answer as to whether it was serious, life-threatening cancer or just a huge pain-in-the-ass fucked-up knee problem.

The surgery went well. The doctors told me I was in the clear. I seriously thought that I didn't have a care in the world, that once the risk of infection was past and I had some physical therapy I'd rejoin the tour. Dave called me two days after the surgery. I was excited to hear his voice. But right away I was weirded out because Prager was also on the line.

"Hey, Bud."

"Hey, Nick."

Mustaine didn't ask me how I was or anything. His first words were, "Hey, we're going to let you go."

"What? Where? Disneyland? Dude, don't fuck around. Now's not the time. I'll be fine in a week they say."

"I don't think you're hearing me clearly," Dave said. "We're letting you go."

I was instantly upset. "Dude, you can't fire me! This is my band, too."

"No, Nick, it's my band, and my mind's made up. I'm not firing you, I'm relieving you of your job."

"You're not relieving me of anything."

I was so fucking rattled I said something like, "The next call you get is going to be from my lawyer," and hung up. I was beside myself with shock. I called the three people closest to me in this world—my sister, my mom and my dad—because they have always been there for me and I knew I could count on them.

First thing my Dad said was, "Thank *God!* I've been waiting for this call!"

Ok, not exactly the reaction I was hoping for at the news of the death of my lifelong dream. It's probably one of the last things you want to hear when you're growing up: that your parents know better than you (well, that or hearing, "Uh, the condom broke"). But parents see through it all and know what's best, don't they? My dad, when it comes to the music business, knows far more than I ever will, and he knew Megadeth was going down the shitter. The band was making less money, selling fewer records, playing smaller and smaller venues, and we were more often in the press because of what was going on in the band rather than what the band was doing musically. Someday, Dad said, I'd be grateful that Mustaine fired me.

By the time the next record was released—or escaped, depending on how you look at *Risk*—I knew Dad was right. Mustaine claims it's a great album. Maybe it is, but, even more than *Cryptic*, it ain't a Megadeth record. Dance beats and electronic shit? That ain't my Megadeth. And I say "my" because I'm a fan, too. I choked when I was told that Billboard's review said Megadeth was "somewhere between Def Leppard and Bon Jovi."

Foreigner, here they come, I thought.

I heard that Huff and Mustaine erased some of Marty's solos and that Dave had replayed them without even talking to Marty. Marty didn't find out until the album came out. I'll bet that sucked. Heartless and heartbreaking. Sort of like being fired over the phone, right, Dave?

Then the band posed with some of the suits from Capitol Records with a fake Gold record. *Risk* sold barely half the number required to go Gold.

Glad my name's not on that bitch.

As for Marty? Well, he quit just three months into the supporting tour and moved to Japan, where he hoped no one had bought a copy of the album, I'd guess. From there (and I'm trying not to be bitter about it, but the truth is the truth), Dave "fired" our mascot Vic Rattlehead and our whole image first, me second, and then lost the whole fucking farm after Marty headed into the house of the rising sunset.

It didn't take long before Megadeth was gone from a major label and couldn't sell even a quarter of a million records instead of the two million we'd begun selling together, and was back to playing theaters and clubs and opening for some of the bands that used to open for us. I didn't talk to Mustaine for a year after he fired me. Piling insult onto injury, he was telling the press all kinds of lies. He fired me because I was fucked up on drugs (*not* true). He fired me because, he claimed, I'd "lied about having cancer."

What the fuck? I think it was around Christmas the following year when he called.

"I just want to see how you're doing?" he said.

"Yeah, I'm doing all right."

"I'm sure you're kind of pissed off."

"Well, I'm not happy about the way things went down, but that's something you needed to do and it was your decision really. It wasn't my decision."

"Well, you can tell people that you left."

"No. I'll tell them that you fired me over the telephone. 'Cause that's exactly what happened."

"Dude, I'm not firing you, I'm relieving you of your job."

"You're not relieving me of anything. The way I see it is that you fired me and that's what I'll tell people when they ask me 'cause that's the honest truth."

Over the phone was just unkind and wrong. I'm on my back in a hospital bed and the guy fucking calls me and tells me he's letting me go? Thanks, brother, you can stop loving me so much any time soon. Nice guy that he is, Junior didn't call me. Not after the surgery, not for a year or something after Mustaine fired me. I never had a problem with Junior and don't want to come off all butt-hurt about it, but, dude, I was hurt. It fucking hurt to just have my whole life for ten years, my best friends, my career, and my passion just shut off like that in one phone call.

I'll be the first to admit that my attitude suffered toward the end. I really wasn't paying attention to Dave or to what he'd say. I was like, "Yeah, right. Whatever." That really pissed him off, and he just had it with my attitude, I think. When I went for the surgery, it was like the green light for him. The first time I saw the guys again was at a club in L.A. I went back and said hello. Jimmy was all uptight. I'm like, "Dude, relax. I'm not here to take your gig or anything." I was thinking, "I mean, I could yank this fucking thing away from you in a heartbeat," but I didn't say it. Jimmy's cool, and I'd known him for years. I sure didn't have any ill feelings toward him. He didn't do anything wrong. But it's weird when you go see a band you've played with for ten years and you see somebody else out there. It's like watching somebody bang your ex-girlfriend, you know? I mean like, "Hey dude, that's not how you do it! You do it like this, bro."

RIM SHOT

LOSING OUR GRIP

I was stoked when it was announced that Megadeth would be supporting Aerosmith on their massive Get A Grip Tour throughout North America in the summer and early winter of 1993.

It kicked off with a great show in Topeka, Kansas on June 2. (Did you know that Topeka, in the native Kansa-Osage language, means a "place where we dug potatoes?" I didn't. Cool, though, eh?)

Looking back, the truth is we were not the right marriage for Aerosmith, though at first it sounded like a good move—us opening for a monster, huge, iconic rock band. From the first night, however, it was doomed. Dave grabbed an Aerosmith t-shirt that had been thrown on stage and wrapped it around the neck of his guitar. Then he took it and held it up to the audience, blew his nose in it and threw it into the pit. Aerosmith drummer Joey Kramer's son was standing on the side of the stage with an "Oh, really?" look on his face.

I'd call that strike one.

We complained about a lot of things right out of the gate: My drums having to be off to the side, the soundcheck, backstage; how long we got to play, or didn't get to play—pretty much everything.

Finally, Steven told us, "You know what? When you guys are the head-liners, you can do whatever you want. But this is our show, and our gig, and this is the way it is. And," he said, zoning in on me, "don't look at my daughter."

Liv Tyler was hanging around the tour, and she and one of her friends had given me a birthday card and a little present one night back-stage. That set Steven off. I honestly wasn't thinking anything! He got right in my shit. "Dude, I know exactly what you're all about because I'm just like you," he said.

Yikes. Strike two?

There was no sexually acting out on that tour, and after Dave's near-fatal overdose six months earlier, certainly no drinking or carousing at the gigs or anywhere in the vicinity of the very sober Aerosmith. No chicks backstage, just us and the wheatgrass juice. I joked that I was glad we got fired because it was really jamming up my style, but that was me making light of how much it sucked to get fired by one of our idols. The guys in Aerosmith are cool, and it's one of the best rock bands to ever come out of America. Like Steven told us, it was their tour, not ours. We were just the opening band and, let's face it, when we were on stage we rocked, but the crowd wasn't there for us. They were like, "Turn that crap off. We want to hear *Toys in the Attic*."

As much as they put up with us for ten dates, the end was swift. Dave did a radio interview and said that he believed Megadeth should be the headlining act, "but we don't mind because everyone knows this is Aero-smith's last hurrah. Aerosmith don't have much time left to live."

Fuuuck. Steven was in the limo with the radio on. "Dave, we'd like to help you out," he said to the press later, "Which way did you come in?"

Strike three, and buh-bye. Fired after just ten shows into a two-hun-dred-and-forty-date tour.

I'm not sure if anyone from Aerosmith even told anybody in our band; all I remember is after a fourteen-hour bus ride to the next show, we pulled into the parking lot and saw Jackyl's bus sitting there. Our road manager came up to us in the restaurant an hour or two later and handed us tickets for our flights home the next day. Replaced by Jackyl.

That stung, dude. I don't know what sucked more: getting fired or seeing Jackyl's drummer play that night in his underwear. And to think we'd given up touring with Pantera for this.

CHAPTER TWO

MUSTAINE REMAINS THE SAME

There aren't many great bands in history that haven't been able to put decades of bitter feuds, even outright hatred, behind them to reunite. Whether that was for a tour, a few shows, or just a single appearance together for charity (Pink Floyd), or a few tunes to thank the fans at the Rock & Roll Hall of Fame (Simon and Garfunkle; The Byrds). Cream, The Sex Pistols, Led Zeppelin, Black Sabbath—shit, even members of the Eagles and Guns N' Roses have been able to put their petty personal crap aside.

Not Megadeth.

It's sad that we've been unable to get the *Rust In Peace* lineup back together for a single show, let alone a one-off tour, at least, for the fans. God knows we've tried several times, and it's always been Mustaine who's pulled the plug. I don't know why he's so threatened by the attention we'd get by reuniting, unless he's worried it would drag down all the work he's done without the core lineup. (When it comes to *Risk*, how could that be a bad thing?)

Both Dave and Junior have said at various times that they want to reunite. Then at other times they claim that they never said that, and

they don't want to ever reunite. We went through the 2004 attempt, which didn't happen, and I admit I wasn't ready.

Chris Grady (lifelong friend and bandmate in Deltanaught):
Those first few years, it was bad. Nick was really depressed and pissed off. Mustaine just ripped his heart out. You'd go into the bathroom, lift up the toilet seat and see these pictures of Mustaine taped to the bottom.

For ages I wouldn't take Mustaine's calls; wouldn't even show up to meet him. Finally, my girlfriend conspired with him to show up at my house. I was upstairs when there was a knock at the door. Terri came up and told me there was someone to see me.

"Who is it?"

"Dave."

"Dave who?"

"Mustaine."

Fuck. I was pissed at both of them. Here's the truth: I wasn't in shape to see him or do anything with anybody, and I'll get into all that in a later chapter. No excuses: I was fucked up and couldn't do the gig. I was still devastated from being fired by Dave five years before.

I think that failed reunion attempt is what helped me get myself straightened out, because I realized that I was in such sorry shape that I couldn't do what I truly wanted to do with my life. All my dreams were going up a pipe. But I tried to save face and, of course, I wanted back in the band. So, I went down to Phoenix for a few days. We got together in the same room and I tried, but I wasn't in any shape to play. I was in total denial then, because that's what addicts do. My ego and pride were far too delicate to have admitted it at the time, so I am the reason the first reunion attempt didn't happen right out of the gate. If everyone's heart had been in it and I'd had Dave's support, and Junior's support, to get healthy and get myself in shape, I would have been able to rise to the occasion and get my shit together. They just didn't have my back to help save me from myself. Nevertheless, I can't blame anyone but myself for not getting the help I needed before I did.

This time, however, I haven't been in such great shape and with chops this good since our heyday.

Dave's now the sole reason Megadeth has yet to reunite. Not to be mean-spirited, but I think his ego and pride are too fragile to handle the attention that Marty and I would get.

I think we're all getting tired of telling the stories over and over again, so here's the final, definitive truth of what happened. Ron Laffitte, who led the band at our height, was back in the fold (briefly, as it turned out). The fans, the critics, even Mustaine and Ellefson had never really stopped talking about the *Rust In Peace* lineup, and Ron made it clear that the path back to greatness was to get the four of us together again. Junior was given the task of talking to Shawn Drover and Chris Broderick, explaining to them that they should find something else to do for the next year, as management was approaching Marty and me about a reunion tour. Shawn and Chris said, "Fuck you," and quit, paving the way for two convenient vacancies.

Mustaine admitted it in several interviews, which surprised me, even if he blamed Ron. "Shawn and Chris quit. They found out about somebody in our organization wanting to make the *Rust In Peace* reunion happen. They got offended. They quit. Things proceeded with Marty and Nick only because I was forced with it because I did not want to do that. When it didn't work out, everybody blamed me, and David Ellefson came to my rescue and said, 'Look, it was my idea. It wasn't Dave. Stop making him the bad guy.'"

Mind you, Mustaine told another reporter that, "I called up Nick Menza first and told him I was going to try to put the band back together, and he said, 'Okay, I'm in.' And then I talked to Marty, and Marty had a bunch of questions that frankly he just didn't need to know the answers to—things about marketing, recording budgets...stuff like that, that was none of his business. And then when I talked to Dave Ellefson, he had concerns too, and after I hung up the phone, I just had this feeling inside me, like, I'm not going to be able to do this. I'm not going to be able to make these guys happy, and I don't think they're going to be able to make me happy."

A different story for everyone.

At the same time, Mustaine began sniffing around for a drum endorsement for me, telling one drum company executive (he copied me and brought me into the email conversation) that Chris and Shawn had quit, but it was no big deal since the fans never really accepted replacements for me and Marty, and will have already forgotten them.

Now, for a little more truth: He did not "call me up." His manager's assistant sent my manager Rob an email.

That was the beginning. The conversation led to me joining the two Daves and Marty for dinner in San Diego with Laffitte. I don't know how serious Marty was. He showed up to the meeting with a camera crew so he could capture it for a documentary that he was doing. It was great to see him and get together, but I don't think he was ever really into it. When I saw Dave, I gave him a big hug.

"Dude, are you all right?" he asked.

"No, I'm not, you know."

It was a really emotional time for me. I hadn't seen him in so long, and I've always considered him a brother. I just don't know why there's always so much competition between us. All the shit the guy's said about me and done to me, I had to put that aside and just be all right with it. And I was.

I always respected him, if not his behavior. Whatever I could do to make it better, I would do. When you're in a band, everybody's in it together or there's no brotherhood. If there's no brotherhood the band simply isn't going to work out. There was none of this last time. No camaraderie, nothing. You need to be able to say, and to be able to hear others say, "I've got your back, bro, no matter what happens. I've always got your back."

It's almost like having a girlfriend, except you've got three of them. Yeah, it's Dave's band, but I always considered it was my band, too, and Junior's and Marty's. A family. Any decisions that were made I always tried to be a part of, and offer my opinion and say, "What if we do it this

Back when it was a brotherhood.

way?" It's not a competition to make a project the best it can be. Who cares which one of us comes up with the ideas, if they work?

We had a jam weekend at Dave's place in San Diego, and it was cool, like we had never parted ways. We know the material and we know how each other played. I'll know those songs forever. Especially the ones I wrote on, but I know the new songs too. You might be a little rusty if you're not doing it every day and you can get lazy and have to work it up at bit, but you never forget that shit. It's muscle memory. I knew going in that we needed to be together for a prolonged period—not just for a few jams. We needed to get together and rehearse for a couple of months to get our vibe back, otherwise it was bound to turn into another cobbled-together, generic, Pro Tools record with no magic.

As I kept pressuring us to get together in person somewhere and do the record like we did *Youthanasia*, all living close together and practicing every day, we kept working on the songs individually, which we sent back and forth via email. We talked about some random date of doing the record, and the subject of recording online came up, because

Marty lives in Japan and didn't seem interested in coming back to America to record.

I was not excited about doing a record that way. Something happens when people play together and you record live. It's magical. I can tell right away when I listen to a band if they're chopped together. I can't stand it. I don't want to listen to that kind of music. For disco and pop and electronic music, it's fine because everything is done to a click and then pieced together. That is what it is, but it's never going to give me goose bumps. There's got to be some feeling to what I listen to and like, some movement where the energy flows. That's one thing that really turned me off coming back this time, but it wasn't a deal-breaker. The deal breaker was Mustaine.

Here, for the first time, you can read it for yourself: the *Rust In Peace* lineup of Megadeth *did* reunite, however briefly and loosely. We went from jamming together to working on quite a few tracks for what would eventually become the *Dystopia* record, though ultimately without Marty and me. We went so far as to begin discussing the public-relations strategy of announcing that Marty and I were back in the band. We were down to negotiating our contracts, talking equipment, wardrobe, and endorsements.

Mustaine wrote to me that he couldn't imagine how enjoyable it would be when we are both able to fully be present in each other's lives, saying that he was completely over the past and wanted to focus on the present because it *is* a present.

I was pretty blown away.

Dave wrote telling me to let him know how he could help make me feel more "back" at home. In another email, Dave wrote to the three of us that we were at the gates of taking our lives and careers to a whole new level with a huge record, huge concerts, and all that comes with it. He also wrote that if we decided not to embark on the reunion, he'd be sad, but would wish us each well.

About twenty-four hours later, he flipped out, stopped answering my calls, blocked my email, and accused my manager and attorney of fucking me over.

I was at a loss to explain it then, and I'm pretty much at a loss now. In the year since, Mustaine and Junior have told wildly different accounts of who wanted the reunion, who's responsible for it flying apart at the seams and, even, the insulting allegation that I was not playing up to par. Well, fuck them and the amps they rode in on for saying shit like that. We had a disagreement over money, plain and simple. Don't lie and say I'm not ready to kick ass on the drums. That's a lame, cheap shot, and it couldn't be more untrue.

When I wanted to come back, my initial thought was I'm worth 25 percent to this band. So is Marty. So is Junior. Fans have wanted the four of us back together for nearly twenty years, and we should be paid accordingly. When Megadeth started out, Mustaine, Junior, Chris, and Gar each owned 25 percent of the band and its profits. That changed only out of greed, which is why Junior ended up in an eighteen-million-dollar battle against Mustaine at one point.

I wanted to come back for the fans because that's what they want. And I didn't want it to reflect on me. I wasn't the one who didn't make it happen, so I've got a clear conscience. I tried. I put it out there. But why would anyone do it for half of what another guy's making? That's not cool. I could go on and on with my side of the story, and they could do the same in the press. Most of my discussions with Mustaine and Junior were on the phone and through text messages, but you can get a decent view of how it played out and fell apart in our emails too. There's no arguing about the core of what's in our actual correspondence. The lawyers say I can't print the exchanges, so I'll do my best to give you the gist of it.

The whole thing started on Tuesday, October 14, 2014, when Laffitte had an assistant reach out to my manager, Rob Bolger, with news that Mustaine was working on a new album and wanted to talk to me.

By December, all four of us had gotten together for that dinner and then Dave and Junior and I jammed for a weekend in Dave's San Diego studio. Dave's son Justice filmed part of it and posted a YouTube video, hiding my face, which really got fans going with speculation that we were re-forming.

We were talking a lot on the phone and texting back and forth, as well as exchanging songs and ideas and plans via email.

Dave told us all that we needed to be ready to make a new record and hit the road opening for another band for three months beginning in August 2015.

Just before Christmas, Dave sent out emails to Junior and me asking us to be discreet with our social media so as not to give away the surprise. He wanted to wait for the moment of maximum impact to announce the reunion.

Dave then started sending out demos to the three of us.

By the first week of January, I'd done drum parts for various songs, including tracks called "I'm An S.O.B.," "Babylonian Ships," and "Emperor's New Clothes."

I had my manager reschedule some recording sessions I'd been booked for so that I could travel to Dave's place in Franklin, Tennessee, to continue writing together and begin rehearsals for a week or so starting on January 16, 2015.

Meanwhile, my manager and attorney received a single communication of an offer from Megadeth management in which I was offered zero money for recording the new album and rehearsing for a tour. Once on the road, I was being offered roughly the same money I'd made as a drum tech twenty years before.

My people made a counter offer, and Mustaine instantly got pissed and pulled the plug on the whole reunion at 8:09 p.m. on January 26, 2015, emailing to tell me he was passing on my involvement and letting me know I could thank my attorney and manager.

Then an email barrage began that lasted for hours in which Mustaine simultaneously insulted me and blamed me before effectively telling me to go fuck myself.

I wrote to him one more time asking him to be reasonable, to let our respective managers and attorneys hammer out a mutually beneficial deal and for us to get down to making awesome music for the fans again, but my email was returned with a Google message that he'd blocked me.

That was it: the beginning and end of the long-awaited and much-heralded Megadeth reunion. I tried to make it happen.

I hadn't wanted to be paid an outrageous amount of money. I would have done it for just enough to not feel insulted. Megadeth grosses anywhere from one hundred thousand to three hundred thousand dollars a night, and Dave was offering me a few grand a month. Commit to an album and tour and not get paid until the tour kicks off? No pay for rehearsals; for recording? Adding further insult is that Mustaine wanted control over what equipment I'd use (because he had an endorsement deal with a drum manufacturer) and, of course, wanted full control over this book you hold in your hands, if he'd even have let it be published at all.

I honestly don't get it, because looking at his emails and the way he was on the phone and in person, with us already working on tunes, sending different takes back and forth and everybody learning the new material, you would have thought it was a done deal, with only the fine details to be worked out.

But they made an offer and wouldn't negotiate when I said I didn't like the deal. I seriously wanted one more show, one more record; one more tour with Megadeth before going back to my future with Chris and Pag in Ohm, because that's where I want to go with new music and new challenges. I have never been sitting here waiting for some shining reunion. If I'm asked again, and Dave's not being a dick with money, I'll do it. I was really into the new material and the possibilities.

We came the closest we've ever come. I was upset that it fell apart at the last minute over a miniscule amount of money, but that's what happened. It's shitty to see it in black and white, but I figured I'd spell it out for you here, because I'm so sick of all of the back-and-forth bullshit and, specifically Mustaine telling our fans one thing in one interview and another thing in the next while the truth is something entirely different.

Yeah, right now I'm pissed off at him. And I have to have attorneys, unfortunately, who are going to bat for me because in the fallout of our last reunion attempt, Mustaine is again holding back my royalties. Unlike every other former member of Megadeth, I don't get paid automatically every quarter. Dave has to personally sign off for the various companies to release my money and when he's butt-hurt at me, he doesn't sign. Of course, I'd rather not air this dirty laundry, but in the almost twenty years since he fired me, sometimes this is the only way I can get him to release my royalties. Once, I actually had to call his house and talk to his wife.

The next day my check arrived by courier. That sucks. It's childish. I've never been Dave's bitch, which, I guess, is why I'm not in the band and yet again, in 2016, we can't seem to agree on the four of us getting back together. Dave's very personable; he's your best friend sometimes. And sometimes he's not.

The truth is that I can never stay angry at him for very long. I probably won't be pissed off at him by the time this book comes out (or next week, for that matter, if he grows up and sends me my royalties). I can't hold onto that negative energy for too long, but I'm telling you how it is right now, for sure. We'll probably end up being better friends now that I'm not back in the band—once the dust settles and he begins allowing my royalties to come through.

Marty finally issued a statement that said, "I think anyone that has something as good as *Rust In Peace* in their history doesn't want to revisit it unless you are going to top it. I didn't see any reason to mess with that. I didn't see a reunion being what it could be and what the fans deserved. If I were to revisit that, there would have to be a reason for me to do that beyond, 'Let's go back and do it again.' That's not a good enough reason."

I will never say never to reuniting with the two Daves and Marty. Whether it's for a record and a tour...just a tour...or even a one-off show at the Rock & Roll Hall of Fame if we ever get inducted. And it's the *RIP* lineup that will get inducted, believe me, though Chris and Gar certainly deserve to be in there too, because the band never would have been there for me and Marty to join if it hadn't been for those two guys.

I won't do a record and tour without getting paid though. I'm not going to go out there and play, seeing Mustaine's ass center stage in front of me and Junior in front of me on the left-hand side, knowing one of 'em is getting eighty percent of what I'm doing, and the other is getting twenty. The fans sure as fuck respect us. If the four of us respect each other, I'm in. We can't wait forever, though. I'm fifty-one, and, yes, that's just a number, but I can't see myself up there at seventy, no matter how great of shape I'm in, playing "Holy Wars."

Who knows, maybe a Megadeth reunion wouldn't bring us back to our heyday, and maybe it would just be a nostalgia trip without the magic. We'll never know if we don't try. I still liked checking out the Beatles' "Free As A Bird," even though John Lennon could only be there in the spirit of a shitty cassette demo tape. And I liked seeing Zeppelin play with John Bonham's son Jason on drums, even if Jason ain't his father and never will be. Neither one those reunions was *Let It Be* or *Song Remains the Same*, but how could they be? Chill out, dude, they were still greater than anybody else in the world could have been. I'm a fan. I'll take whatever I can get. I'm not going to stop dreaming of the four of us playing together at least once more. The fans deserve it, of course, but do you know what's even more? The four of us—Mustaine, Junior, Marty and I—deserve it. We touched the face of greatness, and you never stop wanting to reach for that at least one more time before you hang it up.

"Have a nice life, Nick," he wrote to me at the end of it all.

Life is what you make of it, using your dreams as the raw materials. I have my Mom and Dad and Donia; my two boys, Nicholas and Donte. And I have the honor and challenge of playing in a progressive band with Chris Poland and Robertino Pagliari.

Dude, I have a great life.

RIM SHOT

TWO TWENTIES FOR A TEN

Some of my best stories about my decade with Megadeth end with me saying, "I got in trouble for that."

On one of the American tours, we were traveling in a bus we inherited from Whitney Houston. Rock star buses are full of history, and this one was no exception. Marty and I dug around through the cupboards and underneath the cushions in the back for whatever we might find. And you *never* know what's to be found on a tour bus with any respectable pedigree. But we didn't see this one coming: a bounty of gay porn.

> **Marty Friedman:**
> There was always lots of gay porn around. What could be funnier than that? We used to put gay pics under the dressing room signs of the opening bands. Typical guy stuff. Moronic, but hilarious.

Mustaine takes exception to anything gay—his personal view, and he's been pretty public about it—so I ain't throwing rocks or judging. Marty and I stepped up and did the only thing we could. We got an official, business-looking envelope and mailed a bunch of the gay photos to

Dave's attention at the next hotel we were checking into. It was some fairly conservative stop in the Midwest, just ripe enough and redneck enough for some of our custom-designed rock 'n' roll mayhem.

The clerk at the desk gave Dave the envelope. He ripped it open in front of everybody like it was some mega-million-dollar offer from the record company, and all this gay porn spilled out onto the desk. Dave was *pissed*!

I laughed when Dave complained in his book about it. "You'd offer a beer to a visitor on the tour bus, and when you opened the cooler, sitting on top would be a picture of some guy fucking another guy up the ass.... It was just too perverse, even by the depraved standards of heavy metal." Fucking hilarious!

I don't remember Dave doing anything about our pranks except yelling at me. That's usually what he did, no matter who actually did the deed. Mustaine rarely went for revenge, but when he did, I remember him picking on Marty. One night, he put Bengay in Marty's shoes just before a show. Marty's feet burned the whole night, and he stomped around the stage trying to put out the imaginary flames. He came over to me at one point and yelled, "Dude! My feet are on fire!" Marty and I were co-conspirators when it came to a lot of jokes, but, hey, a cool prank is a cool prank, and it was hilarious to watch Marty thump around the stage. Better him than me!

Marty Friedman:
I faintly remember the Bengay incident, but I really remember when my guitar tech, Tom Mayhew, attached a corncob to my mic stand at a show. I`m sure Dave put him up to that. This was thankfully the extent of my "new guy hazing." I was expecting to be hazed a lot worse, only because I was such a different character from the others. I was a short, skinny Jewish guy with hair that outweighed the rest of my body. I thought I was going to get a lot of "initiation," but I didn't. Even the few times it happened, I felt like I was being accepted, so it was all fun. I think Nick may have had his hazing before I joined the band, and he may have got it worse than I did, as he was probably

more fun to watch react to the pranks than I was. I barely noticed and was probably a boring target. Nick was probably much more animated and more fun to mess with because of that. I think neither of us would have been pranked if the others in the band didn't like us.

In truth, not too many people risked playing pranks on Dave. He didn't respond well to being punked, and he got pissed easily. I mean, even when the wheels were wobbly because of drugs and alcohol, Dave always ran tours like a well-oiled machine, right down to the bus departure. Get to the bus late and it was a ten-dollar-a-minute fine. And you had to ante up as soon as you got on the bus. I was usually the first one aboard. I think I was late just once.

Still, every so often, one or two of us (usually Marty or I) would do something—anything—to break the monotony of being out on the road.

Our tour manager Paul "Skip" Rickert had a good prank that we all got a kick out of. He'd go to the front desks at hotels when they were swamped with guests checking in or out, and he'd rush up and ask, "Can I get two twenties for a ten?" Just about every time, they'd be so busy that it wouldn't even phase them, and he'd get handed two twenties with a quick "Oh sure, here!"

When I first joined Megadeth and was the drum tech for Chuck, I'd set up his drums early in the day to practice. That was a great tour. At one show, I was thinking it was just about time to change his drum heads, but I put it off, instead choosing to get a little mileage out of them. I wrote, "Hit here!" on his snare and drew an arrow to the sweet spot in the center of the head. On the toms I wrote "Hit hard!" and "Don't fuck up!" and all kinds of shit. I thought it was hilarious. Chuck not so much so. He said it distracted him and made him fuck up. Oops. I sure hadn't intended that; I always had Chuck's shit so dialed up for him. I would have never sabotaged some dude to deliberately fuck up his playing.

Still, the tour had some fucked-up moments, such as just before the encore of "Anarchy in the UK" during the May 11, 1988 gig at Antrim, Northern Ireland. Dave drunkenly dedicated the song to the "cause" of "giving Ireland back to the Irish!"

"My words created a parting of the Red Sea in front of the stage," Dave recalled in his book. "Catholic kids on one side, Protestant kids on the other. What they had in common was drunkenness and a willingness to fight at the slightest provocation. And I'd given it to them. The show ended immediately, and we were quickly escorted out of the area in a bulletproof bus."

That sucked, truly. But he did get the song "Holy Wars...the Punishment Due" out of it—the song that I surprised Dave with by knowing note for note before it was even recorded, and which would clinch my gig as Megadeth's drummer.

After Ireland, the band opened for Dio and then Iron Maiden before playing the "Monsters of Rock" festival at Castle Donington in England with Kiss, Iron Maiden, Guns N' Roses, David Lee Roth, and Helloween. We were off the tour after that show, however, because of the substance abuse by Dave and Junior. That sucked.

Soon after, Chuck was fired, and I was brought in as the drummer. That didn't suck.

But pretty quickly, I became the scapegoat for just about all the pranks. Anything that happened off the beaten path was usually my fault, whether it actually was or not. I didn't care. Out there on the road it was just always so tense and uptight.

Juan Alvarez (high school friend):
I was out on tour as Megadeth's videographer for a couple of years; a gig Nick got me. I'll never forget going to Brazil for the first time. Our first night, we got one of the handlers to take us out, and we lit that town on fire, bar hopping and clubbing all night long. It was a blur. The next day we were completely exhausted. We were backstage before the show, and Mustaine comes in and is really pissed off at Nick. He unfolds this newspaper he's carrying, and there's this picture of Nick and me and the headline, "Megadeth Has Landed!" Mustaine was so pissed that it was Nick in the paper and not him. It was hilarious. That's the kind of shit we got into. There was a lot of chemistry between us. If he wasn't making music or sculpting or

painting, Nick was getting into trouble—just the right amount to keep it interesting!

I had *nothing* to do with production manager Tom Mayhew drawing a swastika on Marty's forehead the night before we arrived in Germany on tour! It took forever for him to find out why everyone was glaring at him at the airport. Marty got his revenge when we were flying into Japan and Mayhew's briefcase had "Drugs inside, please check" written on it. Tom was detained as Japanese customs dudes tore his shit apart.

My pranks used to freak everyone out. "What's Dave gonna say?" "What's Dave gonna do?" I was, like, "whatever." Whatever happened and whoever was behind it, I knew Dave would usually come and yell at me for doing something that was "not a good representation of what this band's all about...."

Hey, it's Dave's band, and he has a way of running things. I didn't always agree with it but that's the way it goes.

He was furious with me when I had Nick Menza guitar picks made to throw out into the audience to fans. I had been throwing sticks out at the shows until my tech Bruce Jacobi told me to stop because I was running low on sticks, and at three bucks a pair it was getting a little nuts. I thought, "fuck!" So, I got these picks made with little alien eyes on the bottom that made them look like alien heads and my signature on the back. At a penny apiece it was nothing. At the end of one show, I was in front of my drum riser flicking picks out, and Dave yells, "What the fuck are you doing! That's *our* thing! *We* play guitars and throw out picks!"

When he discovered that I'd had my own made, he threw a fit. The next night, his roadie taped Nick Menza drumsticks all down Dave's mic stand. Dave blew a gasket and knocked over the stand, screaming for someone to take it away. I mean really, he must have laughed for a second. It was pretty hilarious, all these sticks hanging off the bottom. I got absolutely corned for it. The roadie got in trouble for it. I think *everyone* got in trouble for it!

I had wristbands made that said "Menza" on them with the Megadeth *M* and got in trouble for that. I changed the fallout shelter symbol on my bass drums to the radioactive symbol and got in trouble for that. I put it on hats and shirts...I got in trouble for all kinds of shit!

Sure was fun, though.

The best prank I ever played wasn't even on anybody in the band. We were appearing on Letterman one night, and Drew Barrymore was in the greenroom. She said she was going to sing for Dave's birthday. Drew is a riot and really cool. We were laughing and waiting to go on, and I told her she should flash Letterman and give him the best birthday ever.

She did it! (You're welcome, Dave!)

The best prank played on me? No, it wasn't Drew Barrymore, but it was my birthday—my twenty-seventh birthday—in Salt Lake. My tech Rob Corsie had a stripper beneath my drum riser naked during the show. When I looked down, she was inserting a drumstick into her vagina, causing me to lose my way during the first song. Thanks, Rob.

CHAPTER THREE

LITTLE DRUMMER BOY

One would think that I would have had a head start because my Dad is a world-class jazz musician. But it may have actually been my Mom who lit the fire in me to make my living hitting things with sticks.

My dad is Don Menza, one of the last of the great old-school jazz players, and he's my biggest hero. Our family is Sicilian, but Dad was born and raised in Buffalo, where he began playing tenor saxophone when he was fifteen. He studied with the legendary musician and teacher John Sedola.

Stationed in Stuttgart, Dad was in the Seventh Army band with Don Ellis, Leo Wright, Lex Humphries, Cedar Walton, Lanny Morgan, Eddie Harris, and others. After his service, he worked with Maynard Ferguson's Orchestra as both a soloist and an arranger, but he had become unsatisfied with the direction it was heading in and quit.

Between gigs in early 1964 he sent a letter to German saxophonist and bandleader Max Greger, who was huge in Europe. Dad introduced himself and listed what records he could be heard on. Three weeks later, dad and my mom, Rose Marie, were living in Munich.

Though we were there until I was about five, the only things I really remember are that I started speaking German before I learned English; I

once fell and nearly bit my tongue in two; and I once got an idiot mitten caught in an escalator, much to my mother's horror.

All I've ever known is living in Southern California. It's so strange when I've been on tour in Europe and hit the German border and some customs dude says, "Welcome home." Actually, being born in Germany bit me in the ass when I turned eighteen and the German government insisted I do mandatory military service. Thankfully, since Mom and Dad are both American by birth, and I was also an American citizen; it just ended up being a bureaucratic exercise that got solved with some paperwork. The biggest surprise I got the first time I was back there as a teenager in my first successful band was learning that they've got killer beer, each of which is like eating an eight-ounce steak.

Music has always been a huge part of our family life. Mom says that when I was a little kid, just big enough to sit up, she would pull the pots out from the kitchen cupboard in our small apartment in Munich, put them on the floor, hand me two wooden spoons, and I'd bang away. It was great for her, she says, because no matter where she was in the house she could hear that I wasn't getting into trouble.

Sometime shortly before my fourth birthday, and I wish I could remember this, I played drums for the first time. It was at the Montreux Jazz Festival in 1967. No kidding. There's a photo of me sitting there like a pro, playing with my eyes closed, stick in hand, a tom there. It's pretty funny. Dad was playing the festival, so Mom and I were there. My Mom says I crawled up and that, for me, it was like seeing some pots and pans in the form of a drum set. I picked up the sticks as if they were my wooden spoons and started hitting away. Others have said that it was Jack himself who lifted me up and put me on the kit. Either way—I guess it made some sort of impression. Mom says people who had started filing away from the stage turned around to watch me.

Don Menza:

We were living in Munich, and it was the Montreux festival in the spring of '67. I was getting ready to come back to America at the end of four years. I was the leader of the Munich Jazz Ensemble. In those days, the Montreux Jazz Festival wasn't really a jazz festival. It was a competition with all the radio stations in Europe, who would send their jazz ensembles to Montreux and they'd play, and there were judges to decide who would win. We won. And I won the key to the city. It was a great time. Jack (DeJohnette) was giving a drum clinic, and he'd seen Nick walking around the stage. Jack was talking about independence and freedom, and how we're taught not to be so independent. And he saw Nick close by and said, "Come here, Nick" and he sat him on the drums. The audience was like, "What?" All this talk of independence and freedom...and now here's Nick Menza, and he's three years old; and he doesn't know anything about these concepts yet. And Nick picks up the sticks, and we got the picture of him.

We moved to America before my sister, Donia, who's four years younger, was born. Dad joined Buddy Rich's Big Band. Soon after, he recorded the famous solo cadenza on "Channel One Suite" using circular breathing. It has become known as a classic among music educators and musicians alike. Any self-respecting jazz fan will know his compositions "Groovin' Hard" and "Time Check," which he wrote for Buddy. They've become standard repertoire in jazz programs at colleges and universities worldwide. It's totally true for me to say that my biggest hero in music and life is my dad. There was no way I was going to go into jazz when I was a teenager, however, but that's only because that's what Dad does—if he'd been into rock 'n' roll, I probably would have been a jazz head.

It was probably around the time Dad started playing with Buddy that I started to become aware of music as being something that's not always passive—something to be listened to—but something to create.

I became obsessed with drumming. I walked around with drumsticks all the time. I'd sit in class in high school and not pay any attention to the teacher (sorry, Mom!). I spent too much time drawing sketches of drum kits and drum risers and rock 'n' roll stages. And I'd never even been to a rock concert yet.

There are a lot of amazing drummers out there, don't get me wrong, but Buddy Rich was the greatest drummer on the planet. I learned so much just watching him and hanging around. That's all the lesson I needed. Buddy was awesome to me. Super cool. No one could touch that guy. To this day I've never seen a drummer who even comes close to him. If you watch Buddy Rich and still think you can play the drums, you'd better step back and watch him again and think about it. There were things he could do that I wouldn't even try. He was a natural freak on the drums. He once had me to hold a paper towel up between my hands and he did drum rolls on it and didn't even rip the paper. That was his control, like stopping the stick in mid-air. He's my all-time drummer and mentor. I loved it when he appeared in drum battles. Buddy wiped the stage with anyone. He'd laugh about it too. I loved when he'd appear on the Jerry Lewis Telethon every Labor Day. His drum battles with Jerry were hilarious.

My Dad played a lot of those telethons, and one year when I was a teenager I was there backstage with Jerry and Ed McMahon. I lit up a joint and Jerry got so stoned he couldn't go out and do his next segment. I remember Ed just sitting there laughing like he did on the Carson show, and Jerry said to me, "What was that shit? Paraquat?"

Nah, it was bad ass skunk weed. We were all seriously fucked up, man.

I got to go on Buddy's bus once with Dad for a trip up to a show in San Francisco. Buddy came on and asked me if I could roll. I said, "Drum roll?" He said, "No! Joints!"

Sure could!

I've heard some absolutely awesome Buddy Rich stories. He was always so kind to me, but his temper was legendary. Buddy had a reputation of being hard on his band members. He was notorious for neglecting to introduce the players—instead having them each stand for a moment of recognition. I heard that once somebody in the front row

yelled out, "Hey, Buddy, how about introducing the band members?" Without missing a beat, Buddy fired back, "That's not necessary. They all know each other by now."

That's Buddy. He never missed a beat of any kind.

I heard that in 1986, when he was being wheeled into surgery for his malignant brain tumor, he was asked if he was allergic to anything. Buddy responded, "Only two things: country and western."

Fans still leave drumsticks instead of flowers where his grave is located at Westwood Memorial in L.A.

My first-ever drum memory is at my parents' house. We lived on Riverside Drive in the Valley, and my Dad used to have rehearsals there. He had a drum set for guys to play. I thought it was so rad when I learned how to hit the bass drum and the crash cymbal at the same time. That's all I would do! My dad would come in annoyed at the repetition and go, "What are you doing?"

Don Menza:

I really had no expectations of him, or his sister, being involved in the music business. I really didn't encourage Nick in the beginning, but when I saw that that's what he had, and that he was interested, I went along with it. I tried to point him in the right direction, because what you think you're going to do may fall out and that's it, you've got all your eggs in one basket, and that's not going to work. And that's exactly what happened. He wanted to be a rock 'n' roll star. I said "Ok, whatever." I didn't try to dissuade him. If nothing else, he's my son, and above all else we're friends. I know the business fairly well and how unpredictable it can be. He had a lot of talent. Let it go; it's your life. You'll see. And he did. Nick as a teenager rehearsing in the basement—it got to be a pain in the ass.

Nothing else sounded so cool to me. Not the snare, not the tom, just the bass and the cymbal.

As I learned more of the cool sounds I could make every day after school, I started getting more serious about it. One of the first things I did was take a can of flat black paint and spray the whole set. It had blue sparkles, and I thought it looked so uncool. My Dad was pissed. "Man! What the hell did you do to the set?" I said, "I painted it! It looks cool doesn't it? It rocks!"

The better I got, the more I started to learn every one of my favorite songs. I used to jam to a lot of Elton John, Boston, Styx, Rush, Van Halen, Aerosmith, Kansas, and Tom Scott records. *Tomcat* was an album I used to jam to a lot.

Zeppelin was the most influential band to me. *Physical Graffiti* was probably my favorite album to drum to, though I love *Presence* too. "Candy Store Rock" is pretty cool. "Black Dog" is a difficult Zeppelin song to learn. Bonham played straight through, odd-meter part, simple beat, getting the feel of it. "Nobody's Fault" is pretty tough to play too. Mostly, however, I had a lot of trouble with my favorite Zep song of all time, "Achilles Last Stand." The fills are blisteringly fast. That was hard for me to figure out, and, of course, mastering that Bonham groove is no easy thing. It's such a badass song. I used to go to sleep at night listening to it on a turntable. I would get up in the middle of the night and put it back on the beginning of the track again and again because I didn't want to listen to "For Your Life" or "Royal Orleans."

I used to come home from school and play "Achilles Last Stand" over and over again trying to lock it down. One day, my Dad came into the basement and said, "Man, if I hear this song one more time I'm taking away your records, your drums, and the stereo."

"But Dad, I've almost got this song wired!"

"No I've got the song wired, and I don't even play drums," he said. "I don't want to hear it anymore."

My dad hates Zeppelin. He thought they were out of tune and obnoxious. He's into opera and jazz. I can see why he didn't like it. He has perfect pitch and, let's face it, there's some Zeppelin stuff that isn't in tune, like "Stairway To Heaven." From start to finish, those guitars are not in tune with one another.

He had a big sign in the basement that said, "Electronic Noise, Who Needs It?"

I put one up above the drums that said, "Help Stamp Out Opera."

Mom was totally cool with it all, though, and she told me, "Just wait until your dad goes out and then you can play it."

I can't overstate how important Led Zeppelin was to me. The very first time I saw *Song Remains the Same* was in a theater in Studio City. The movie wasn't even finished, and I had decided that I was going to be a drummer, join a band, and go on the road and play for people just like I saw Bonham doing it. It was a total epiphany.

The next morning, my Mom came to wake me and tell me it was time to go to school. I told her that I didn't need to go to school anymore.

"No? You need to go to school and get smart and learn things."

"No, I need to play drums!"

Every kid says that, but only a handful follow through. I know how lucky I am that I had so many amazing influences around me. Dad took me to the studio all the time when he was doing sessions, along with many of the shows he was playing. Besides Buddy Rich, some of the greatest drummers ever stopped by the house to see Mom and Dad. When they were hanging out, they would give me little tips. Steve Gadd; Louie Bellson—all just awesome. Bellson, who was the pioneer of the double-bass kit, sent me a drum set as a gift when I was about twelve years old. A beautiful surprise. I still have it.

Chuck Flores had me reading beats and showed me some trippy little hand exercises. I took a couple of lessons from Nick Cerolli who played with my Dad a lot, and who put out a speed and endurance book of rudimentary snare stuff.

It was all cool, but I wanted to play music, not fuck around with lessons.

I got some drum tips from Joe Porcaro, who told me I wasn't holding my sticks the right way and said he'd have to start at the beginning with my training. Well, that wasn't going to work for me.

I believe in whatever works for you. If you can really play your instrument, go for it. Don't get me wrong, Joe is a great dude and an amazing drummer whose late son Jeff, the Toto drummer, I was close to. But lessons weren't for me. I pretty much single stroke; I don't play any doubles. Usually, my left hand will pop out, but single is louder. I'm a Neanderthal drummer. I play loud and hard. I try to break things! Who else can make a living hitting things with sticks?

For a time, however, the idea of lessons was as regular a thing as great food in our house. Dad wanted me to go to Berklee. I said, "That would suck! No, Dad, that's not happening. Please! Dad, don't send me to Berklee."

I was totally terrified of being sent to Boston. Most people would love to go to Berklee, but not me. You ask him, that's exactly what I said. God, it was like my worst nightmare.

I know that it was my Mom and Dad trying to help me as much as they could toward my dreams. They supported me in everything I did, and of course music was just a natural thing, since there was music going on in our house what seemed like 24/7. Believe me, I've heard it all. Dad's no rock 'n' roll fan, but he's very hip and up on what's contemporary. He's a great arranger, composer, and writer.

Don Menza:

Nick was always into music. When he was a baby, he used to cry when it was time to go to bed, and we'd play this Spanish flamenco record, which always worked. It was funny the things that touched him. Later he was always drawn to rock 'n' roll. But he paid attention to what I was doing. As he got a little older, there were times he'd come with me to set the big band up, stay all night and look at all the beautiful girls.

My mom's funny, though. She was always so stoked to come see me play. All that ever mattered to her was that I be happy. She and Dad and Donia came to as many Megadeth shows as they could. Mom always told me she thought I was going to hurt myself playing the way I did in Megadeth. Any decent drummer in a heavy metal band is working from beginning to end. That's why you play drums in a band like that, because that's how you want to play. You don't want to be kicking back, playing brushes and never breaking a sweat—you want to push it as far as you can. I did actually get hurt playing with Megadeth one night. During a rehearsal, one of my sticks shredded, and a splinter flew up and hit me in the eye. My instinctual reaction was to rub it, and I pushed the splinter further in. I ended up wearing an eye patch for a while. Some doctor told me I should wear safety goggles when I played. I think that's pretty much the stupidest thing I've ever been told. Like that was going to fucking happen.

Don Menza:

We went to see Nick play as many times as we could. Dave Mustaine asked me one time, "Tell the truth, when Nick started playing, did you ever think Nick would wind up like this and being so successful?" I looked Dave in the eye and said, "Absolutely." Megadeth changed when Nick joined. Rolling Stone had a big article about that—finally getting a drummer that makes some sense. My name's in that article, too! Papa made the Rolling Stone, ha! You know, I'm not into all that but I remember one night I had a friend staying with me, and I asked him, "Hey, what are you doing tonight? I got passes." We had our earplugs and went to the show at the Hard Rock. He's not into that stuff, either, but when we left, he said, "Wow! That was tight! That was...surgical." And it was. I was always impressed.

Dad has always been such a support; he willingly showed up at the studio when Marty Friedman and I were working on Marty's solo record *Scenes*. Dad played shakuhachi, which was awesome. Marty was so stoked. "Your Dad knows how to play shakuhachi! No way!"

My dad's a blast in the studio. I went on a lot of sessions with him when I was a kid. He's no bullshit; he gets in and handles it. Two passes, and he's got it. He can play anything on the tenor sax—the last of a dying breed. He played sax on a song called "The King" that I did with a few friends in a band we call Deltanaut.

He needs to write a book, a huge catalogue of people he played with. Henry Mancini, boy did that guy write some songs! Dad played with him a ton. He was the nicest guy. I loved him.

Me, Donia, Dad, and Mom.

I think rad people come from cool parents who support their kids in whatever they do—as long as it isn't illegal!

I have to say I'm so grateful to my mom and dad and Donia. I had a very happy childhood. I'm from a functional family! I think that's why I never got into too much trouble. I was a good kid. Summers were spent riding our bikes around into the backyard and right into the swimming pool—fun, harmless stuff like that. I was sent home from school once for wearing a Pro Drum Shop t-shirt that had a "We're No. 1" on the back. The No. 1 was a middle finger. The principal said that wasn't acceptable.

I think the most trouble I got into was when I skipped school for two weeks. All of a sudden, Mom got this call from the principal's office: "Where's Nicholas?"

Oops. I'd been leaving the house every school day and going to hang at a friend's house. I was hiding. For quite a while, I had been getting ripped off by this kid from the 18th Street gang in the Valley. He was taking my lunch money from me. Finally, I said, "Fuck it!" and attacked him with some aluminum drumsticks. I knocked him unconscious. That day, there were twenty gang members waiting for me outside the school. I got home safely but then wouldn't risk going back. I didn't tell anyone except for a few friends. But I had to go back to school. I managed to avoid getting my ass kicked. Finally, one of the gang members came up to me and asked me what was up. I told him that I just couldn't take getting ripped off by this kid anymore. He said, "Ok. Can you drive?"

I said of course I could drive.

He said, "All right, we're going for a ride." I thought they were going to really hurt me. You know, drive me down to the railroad tracks and beat the shit out of me. But they didn't. I drove, and they told me where to go. As we got onto a side street, they pulled out guns and started blasting out of the open windows, and they told me to step on it. No one got hurt, and they seemed to lose interest in me after that. But it was fucked up. From then on, the only gangs I'd be around were the ones whose neighborhoods measured from one side of a stage to the other.

A BAD NIGHT IN EUGENE, OREGON

I think it's just human nature that experiences with the greatest shock value are the ones that we remember most vividly. This applies, of course, to all my years with Megadeth. I remember that massive show in Rio well and fondly. But I don't remember too many of the other great shows. First of all, there were so many of them. When we were on tour, we played an absolutely grueling schedule. There would be ten shows in a row, moving from city to city by bus, then a flying travel day before another ten shows in a row. There were no days off. That was another one of Dave's rules. "There are no days off," he always said. "There are only non-performance days."

He wasn't kidding. He was adamant about that. Our tour books, comprehensive guides that told each member of the band and crew where we were supposed to be at any given time, in what city, what hotel, with all the phone numbers we needed, actually listed "Non-Performance Day" in the calendar on days we didn't have a show. It didn't say "Day Off."

It was terrible on the crew. Those dudes would be pretty torn up. It wasn't as bad on us, and I actually disliked days off. I just spent money and got bored. Once you've been to these cities all over the world a few times it's like, "Yeah, I've seen that already. Can I go home now?"

I've got to say, though, it made us one of the greatest live bands out there. Metallica may have gotten bigger than us, but they couldn't play as well as we did. So, the great shows tend to all blend together in my memory. But the bad ones, fuck, those stand out.

Probably the worst was in Eugene, Oregon in February of 1993. That was definitely not a good night for us. Dave was supremely fucked up on some heinous mix of drugs and alcohol. As soon as we came on, we went into "Sympathy for Destruction," and he was playing "Peace Sells." I looked over at Junior like, "Are you fucking kidding me?"

I think it was about the third song when the barricade at the front of the stage snapped with a thunderous *bang*, and kids began rushing the stage. It quickly turned into a riot, with people beating each other while there were a few kids trapped under the fallen barrier. People started throwing bottles. Security was trying to beat people off the stage. We were hustled through the back of the stage and onto the bus, which immediately took off. There was a stream of kids beside and behind us, pelting the bus with bottles and shit. It was completely out of control—very scary.

Dave went to his bunk and tossed back a bottle. Of Valium. We didn't even make it to the hotel before we had to detour to the hospital. He wasn't just passed out. Sometime after they rolled him into the ER, we were told he was clinically dead. He was in a coma for a week and then still in the hospital for another week before he was well enough to go to rehab. The rest of us went home, just a month into a long tour with Stone Temple Pilots opening for us. It sucked all around. Dave had to issue an apology, and we had to return the ticket money. What made it even more disappointing was that we were booked to play the famed Budokan arena in Tokyo, something we'd all seriously been looking forward to.

Thankfully, however, no one was seriously injured or killed at the show, and as Junior said at the time, it was probably the most disappointing time for us. If it hadn't have happened and Mustaine hadn't gone to rehab, he probably would have been another rock 'n' roll drug casualty, found dead in a hotel room on that tour.

The bad times are hard to forget.

CHAPTER FOUR

NORTH HOLLYWOOD HIGH

The first real band I saw live was bound to suck, I thought, because they were playing at my high school.

"They're called Boston," someone said.

Great. All this and a lame name, too.

Dude, Boston was so awesome! That was a fucking rock show. There was nothing lame about them. They kicked ass. The bass and the sound that they had was so intense. I don't think that anyone had a clue what was going on there. I went right out and bought their record after that. I thought their cover was cool—the guitar flying upside down and the flame. Every song on that record is huge.

That was my first concert. That was the first time I embraced my Buddhist chant: "I need to be doing that up there, not that guy. That guy sucks." "That guy" was whoever was playing drums; it didn't matter who it was. In this case, it was Sib Hashian, and, of course, he didn't suck. It simply became my mantra for seeing myself up there on stage instead of out in the audience.

High school is the training ground for later life, and the first bands I was in were the equivalents of my college degrees. One of the first short-lived bands was a cover band called No Mercy, named after the singer, Mercy Baron. She studied at the Musonia School of Music and was friends with guitar prodigy Randy Rhoads, whose mother ran the school. We did an all Top 40 set list of Bowie, AC/DC, Zeppelin, Van Halen, Ozzy, Queen, Billy Squier, and on and on.

We learned a whole whack of covers and did a little recording, but the band never actually played live. I tell people my first band lasted for a weekend, which wasn't far from the truth. But, significantly, it was the first time I played with guys who would become lifelong friends and musical peers; John "Gumby" Goodwin on guitar and Darwin Ballard on bass.

Gumby and Darwin were in a band called Emeralde with a drummer named Steve Klong. He was a good drummer, and Gumby would become one of the most important friends and musicians in my life. All of us in the neighborhood would go out and see Emeralde play. I was a fan. I thought they were rad, progressive, a supercool band. It was all original stuff with a sort of Styx, Kansas, and Rush kind of vibe. Before long, I started helping them out, moving stuff at gigs, setting up the drums, and anything they might need a hand with. It was inevitable that I started jamming with them, and one day Gumby said, "Hey, why don't we start another band with you in it?"

I don't really remember how it came about, how I came into the band and Steve left, but I got the gig as the drummer. There was Darwin Ballard on bass and Steve Ely on guitar with Gumby and a dude named Dave Myers on vocals. Emeralde was a rad band, and we had a great

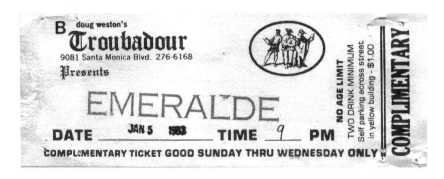

following. We played The Troubadour, which was really exciting and got a great response from crowds and critics alike.

The band was hot, and the momentum was constant. Pretty soon, we caught the attention of Randy Rhoads' older brother Kelle, who'd been the drummer in Randy's first group and who was now looking for a band. Kelle is a great dude and an intense singer.

> **Kelle Rhoads:**
> There was something absolutely magical about Nick. I was never on stage with a guy like him before, and I've never been on a stage with someone as powerful as him since. If you were lucky enough to be in a band with him, and you were smart, you let Nick shine through. That's probably the biggest mistake Mustaine has ever made in his life. Mustaine may have been the singer and the front man, but Nick was always the star.

He was funny and put on a fabulous show, and he had some solid industry connections. He didn't want to be in a band that didn't have his name, so we changed our name to Rhoads, got management and that was it: I was at the grown-ups' table.

There couldn't have been a more righteous place for me to pop my recording cherry than Sound City. That legendary studio has the best drum sound in the world. They won't even repaint the main room's walls because no one wants to fuck with the magic of the acoustics in there. I swear anyone's drums sound awesome in that room. Just set 'em up and string up two overheads, and you're in heaven. Recording in there gave me my first hands-on experience on what drums should sound like in a studio and on stage—lessons I've taken to heart ever since. I was in heaven.

Our management was murky and questionable, which is the standard story, isn't it? You can't do anything without somebody running the books, and you can't find anybody to run the books who isn't crooked. The game is to find the least corrupt manager you can. Our guy was somewhere in the middle on that scale, I think. He got a German label,

From L to R: Darwin Ballard, me, Steve Ely, John "Gumby" Goodwin, and Kelle Rhoads.

Interchord Records, to come in to support the album, which was called *Into the Future*. A decent amount of money started flowing for us. We had amazing gigs up and down the coast and landed the opening slot on a Foghat tour, which was an absolute riot. We played a bunch of bars with mechanical bulls, with shit-kickers looking at us and not knowing what to think. We were one of the first bands to have a laser show at our gigs. We played loud! It pissed off the road manager of Foghat, who was always telling us to turn down. We'd do it, too, at soundcheck. Then we'd come out blasting. I started those shows with a drum solo to let the audience know we meant business and to absolutely get their attention. We killed wherever we played. If it was disrespectful to the opening act, dude, who cares? We weren't playing for them; we were playing for the crowd. It ain't show *friends*, as they say, it's show *business*. Some shows at The Troubadour were epic. Everybody wanted to come and see Randy's brother Kelle. We were often better than Foghat.

John "Gumby" Goodwin (lifelong friend, bandmate):
It was a big deal for the band. Everyone was in a great mood. We were rehearsed and ready to go. We did our first gig in San Diego at the Bacchanal Club. Everyone was subdued, and we played a tight, but reserved, set. By the time we got to Sacramento—my hometown—we were rock gods! I remember the soundcheck there and Foghat's very English tour manager smugly suggesting we turn way down. We turned down, like a micrometer, then finished our soundcheck. When you play on stage with Nick Menza, you need some serious amplification firepower to match the guy's natural volume, let alone his mic'd-up kit. After the show in the dressing room, the Tea Bag came in, and he was mental mad screaming at us. We were pretty sheepish, since this hard-ass English band known all over the world had taken on an unknown group of twenty-year-olds and given us a chance. He came around and told us that we "were pretty good, but don't be too good." It was a great tour. Nick's solo was like a call-and-answer with the crowd, and they loved it. Nick came off stage every night like an athlete who had just won the match. He had such a good feel. He could play anything randomly out of his head, and people loved it. As a drummer, he engaged the crowd like he was the front man.

The record came out in Europe but not America, so nothing came of it. It was all fucked up. Dad helped with the mixes, but I don't think anyone even knows where the masters are. It would be worth resurrecting. The playing is really good. The final sound was frustrating, considering the songs were tight and we'd recorded it at Sound City. We had a tour offer of some festivals in Europe and I know Kelle accepted, but they, too, never materialized. The only substantial thing to happen over there was a single show in Germany on a rock television program called *Rock in Rock TV*. I fell in love with the host, this awesome blonde named Christina Rotig. She was my first love affair on the road, and she totally broke my heart.

I hadn't been back in Germany since I was born. The first thing I did was go to a bar and get this great big ball of hash for about ten marks. I went back to the hotel and knocked on Kelle's door with a big smile. We sat in his room making can pipes and getting unbelievably stoned. We watched the sun come up.

It was the first time I drank European beer, which was a whole new experience. The stuff was like a meal in a glass. My pee came out orange. I panicked, thinking there was something wrong with me. I remember playing the show was brutal because we had to play along to the record. It's one thing for guitarists or the singer to fake it, but it ain't so easy for the drummer, because we can't actually fake it. We either play or we don't, and it's difficult to play drums when the band isn't really playing. You gotta remember exactly how you played. There's nothing lamer than when you're playing on the ride and all of a sudden it's the high hat or there's a fill going on and you're just sitting there.

It was a great experience, though, being out on tour with Kelle and the band. He's an enormously talented singer and charismatic front man. He teaches now at the Musonia School of Music, which his mother Delores Rhoads started back in the late 1940s. It also became a small museum honoring Randy after he was killed.

The band lasted two or three years but finally collapsed due to mismanagement and neglect. Everyone in the band got along great, but I think there was just such a disappointment with what had happened with the record and being so let down by our management that the whole experience was deflating, so we went our separate ways.

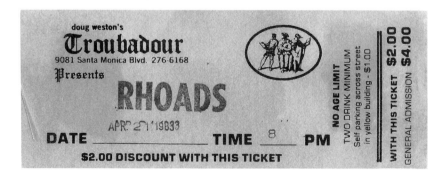

From the ashes of Emeralde, Gumby and I formed a new group he called The Green.

> **John "Gumby" Goodwin:**
> The Green was the band where Nick really began to shine. We liked to just jam and see what happened because Nick led these sessions. He controlled the beat. We all loved the changes he took us through, and we relied on him to do it. Nick was so musical, more than any other drummer, and he applied his songwriting to pounding the drums. He could be so free and easy and had such a feel for music, and he fed off the crowd's reaction. You know—an artist! He could be so dynamic, and that's how Nick played when nobody fucked with him and just let him do his thing. If you had Nick Menza in your band, you show him off, man!

We began writing awesome originals and doing Zeppelin covers, which I loved playing; they always got the audience off. A Robert Plant sound-alike named Gary Mac came in on vocals, and we started gigging at The Country Club and the Whisky. We pushed hard and had great gigs and wrote some amazing material, but the band just never rose above the competition of the day, which at that time was probably as fierce as it will ever be in L.A. I really don't see things ever getting to that rabid a point ever again. There just aren't enough great players these days.

The Green was a great band, but it fell apart for no reason other than deflated dreams, which is a pretty valid reason for packing it in, if you've ever been there.

Gumby and I were at a loss as to what to do next. We were sitting around his house one day when we found ourselves inspired, and we ended up writing a whole album for our next project. I said, "Let's all get dressed up as skeletons and come out on stage and be this total band of dead-undead rockers!" Gumby's cool, and he'll go along with an idea until it either proves itself or it doesn't.

With Gumby in London.

I wanted to call the band Skeletor but it turned out that Marvel comics owned that name, so I started calling it Von Skeletor. We couldn't find a vocalist. We auditioned all these lame singers. It really irritated me, having to hear all these knuckleheads.

Juan Alvarez:
It was all Nick's idea. He and Gumby and I were hanging out at Nick's house, swimming in the pool or riding our bikes, and he comes up with this idea that he wants to start a band based on a cartoon character, this Skeletor guy. At first it was like, "That's kinda stupid, dude." But Nick always had a way of convincing you that it doesn't sound so dumb after a while, after he'd kept thumping at you. Gumby wrote a bunch of music for it, and Nick decided he'd be the singer, so we had to find a drummer—only there was nobody who could touch Nick on the drums. It seemed like a really easy thing to do. We recorded an album, but the really disappointing thing was that we never got to play out. Right then things really started to take off for Nick.

That's the only band I ever fronted, playing guitar and singing instead of playing drums. We had a cool thing going on with that for a second, and we recorded a privately financed record we called *Injection of Death*. It was some dark shit. Steven and Slash from Guns N' Roses were hanging out a lot with us then, and they were way into it, telling us we needed to get out and take it on the road. But we never did. Looking back, I'm surprised that Slash and I never did anything together.

I left Von Skeletor when I got a chance to join Slayer. Dave Lombardo had quit the band about a month before they were set for a European tour in support of *Reign in Blood* because, he said, he wasn't making enough money.

Slayer had an open audition in L.A. for a replacement. It was one of those classic cattle calls, with drummers lined up with their sticks and high hopes whether they had the talent or not. I was determined to get the gig, but I wasn't sure I could play fast enough with the wooden beater balls I had on my pedals. I changed them to the felt ones. When I sat down after saying "Hi" to the guys, we launched into "Raining Blood." Almost immediately, guitarist Jeff Hanneman laughed and said, "Whoa, whoa, whoa dude, that's way too fast. Chill out! Relax man, we know you're excited."

The tour manager was there and said, "Wait, did I just hear you say 'too fast'?"

"Yeah," Tony, the bass player, said. "This guy's off to the races here. Just mellow down dude."

We started again a little slower, and after we were done with the song, the guys looked at each other, and Tony said, "You're our guy."

Given the competition to earn the throne in Slayer, I thought for sure I wasn't going to make the cut. But that was it: I came out blazing and got the gig in one song. I was on my way. I was so pumped to get the gig that I dropped everything else I was doing for a crash course in all things Slayer. I spent weeks learning all their songs and rehearsing with them. Then Dave Lombardo came back into the band after he heard that they'd replaced him, and I was out. I didn't know it at the time, but Rick Rubin, who had produced the album, repeatedly called Lombardo to return. He initially refused, but then Tom Araya's little brother told me that Lombardo had started coming down and hanging out outside our rehearsals. He'd apparently listen outside the door, splitting before we came out. I guess he got nervous because they'd found another drummer who could pull it off. I made him nervous! Just before the tour was supposed to start, the guys told me that Lombardo was rejoining the band. I didn't even get paid for my month or so with them and for putting in all the time. That sucked, but I understood him coming back.

I hadn't made a name for myself yet, so Lombardo didn't know who'd nearly taken his place until a few years later when we were out on the Clash of the Titans Tour. I was sitting in a bar with him and casually said, "Dude, those songs of yours are hard. It was hard work for me to learn that shit."

He was like, "Wait! That was *you*? You were the guy? Why didn't you tell me?"

He was dumfounded. It was cool. I didn't begrudge him for coming back—he'd helped start Slayer, after all—but at the time, it was a mix of irritation and humiliation and, well, pride that I'd made Dave Lombardo nervous. I read later that Hanneman said that at the time, the band was making a conscious decision to slow everything down, which they did on the next record, *South of Heaven*, by doing things like introducing acoustic guitars to the mix. There was no way they could top *Reign in Blood*, so they had to go another direction for their next record. Well, I guess I slowed down enough to get the gig, but Rubin wanted Lombardo back, and he came back. Time again for chanting my Buddhist chant, with that certain goal in mind, "I need to be doing that up there, not this guy. That guy sucks."

For a short time, I was in Joe Floyd's band Warrior, which had changed its name to Cold Fire. We played around a bit, but the whole vibe was sour because of constant problems from their record label, which had dropped the band.

While all this was going on, I started trading on the reputation I was gaining from Rhoads and The Green, and I began landing studio gigs.

I think I played on more than 200 sessions in a very short time. I'm on all kinds of stuff. I played with some pretty big popular bands where the drummer sucks, and it would surprise you, but I'm bound by confidentiality agreements that I can never go public. There were so many studio gigs that I don't even know all the songs I'm on. There were some where no vocals had been done yet—they just brought me in to lay down the drums because their drummer couldn't fucking hack it in the studio.

I'm on everything from R&B and gospel to funk and metal, right up to a session I did with John Fogerty. He was amazing in the studio—extremely inventive and creative and willing to try anything to get a great drum sound. John didn't give a shit about "rules" of recording, which was awesome.

Cinderella is another band where it was me on drums. Sometimes a song will come on the radio and I'm like, "Did I play that? I might have played that." To be honest, it's kind of hard to tell when you're playing to a click track and a scratch guitar and bass and you don't hear anything finished. I did *a lot* of ghost playing. I'd come in—to studios everywhere in the Valley and over in Hollywood—and there would be a click track. I'd play one or two takes, get paid, thanks, see ya. Usually I'd only meet the producer and engineer. That's the way it works.

The record labels, and especially the bands, don't want their fans knowing that I played on it and am not their poster boy. I get it. You're out there trying to market a band, and when people find out that I'm the guy playing the drums it's like, "Oh, no wonder they suck live."

Many producers do that. The band comes in and plays, and after they leave, the producer has the session guys come in to play the shit right and make it real. The next step is pushing it to radio to see if people like it. If they do, you have to go out and support it, so you're good for one tour in every market. If the band can't produce or put on a good show, then that's it. Here today; gone later today. It's ruthless.

One day, my chant seemed to pay off. I got a call from Neil Schaeffer, who we all knew as the best sound guy in town. He'd been doing house sound at the Country Club, where we all played in whatever bands we were in at the time, but he'd moved onto doing sound for Megadeth on the *Peace Sells* tour. Neil called me one day and said, "They're looking for a drummer. Do you want to play for them?"

I said, "Fuck yeah! I'm doing jack shit here in L.A."

Neil told me to go down to a show at the Santa Monica Civic Auditorium and hang with the band. Everybody was cool. Dave was like, "This is the little drummer boy? Got any pot?"

"Yeah." I pulled out a joint, and we smoked in the bathroom. Dave said he was getting rid of Chuck Behler because Chuck was blowing it. Nothing came of that first meeting, but I saw them all again a few months later and was offered the job of being Chuck's tech. I jumped at the chance, because I thought (and everyone told me) that it wouldn't be long before he was fired. Nothing against Chuck; he's a really nice guy and a great drummer.

In a bizarre twist of the fate that always seemed to bring us together, Gumby was Dave Mustaine's guitar tech by this time.

I learned a lot in a very short time. You have to if you're a drum tech, guitar tech, or whatever, and you also have to know how to tech for anybody in the band.

There was no sense of when Mustaine might fire Chuck, though sometimes it seemed like "today's the day."

I'd made the grave mistake of telling my parents that I was getting in a band playing drums, which if it wasn't exactly a lie wasn't yet true. I couldn't tell them I was a roadie when that job dragged on from a few weeks to a few months.

I found myself not just teching for Chuck but tuning the guitars and part-time stage-managing. Then, finally, I was driving the truck.

"What am I doing?" I said to myself. "How do I get out of here?"

At first, I was pumped to be in the Megadeth organization. But after a while, I didn't want to tell anyone. I was in my humble stage.

The next thing you know, Dad shows up at one of the gigs in Europe, and I'm pushing a road case across the stage.

"Hey, man, what are you doing?"

I had to tell him that I didn't have the drumming job yet. He was all vibed at me for not telling him the truth.

"I didn't want to tell you," I said, "But I'll be the drummer soon."

"Oh, you're full of shit, Nick," he said.

Top: Nick hiding on a shelf below one of his father's saxophones. Munich, Germany, 1966.

Bottom left: Nick's first drums—pots and pans his mother, Rose, put on the floor for him. Munich, Germany, 1964.

Bottom right: If it made a noise, it was Nick's friend. His first guitar. Munich, Germany, 1967.

Top: Nick's first professional photo shoot, which he loathed. Thereafter he either put on a goofy face or looked at the camera expressionless.

Bottom: Teenage Nick practices in the basement.

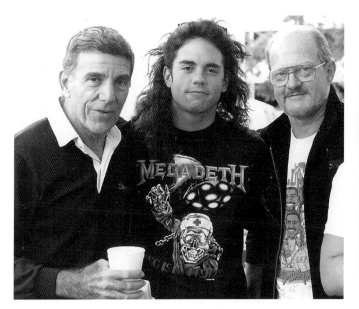

Top left: Nick with his idols, drummer Louis Bellson, and his father, Don Menza, circa 1987.

Top right: Buddy Rich and Nick backstage at the Playboy Jazz Festival, June 1980, at the Hollywood Bowl.

Bottom: Nick with his mother, Rose, and his sister, Donia.

Nick in a pre-tour publicity shot for *Countdown To Extinction* with his new Greg Voelker Rack System drum kit, which he would make famous.

Top: Megadeth surrounds beloved wardrobe wizard Dawn Brumley, backstage somewhere on the *Rust In Peace* Tour.

Bottom: Chilling by the pool before their career-highlight gig at the Rock In Rio Festival, January 23, 1991.

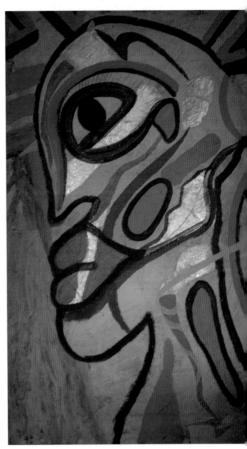

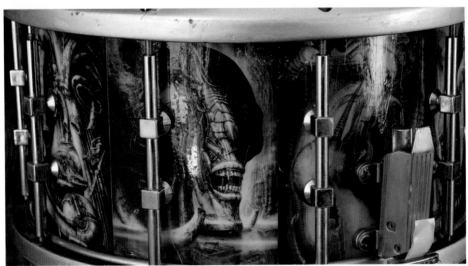

Top left: "Needle Man," one of Nick's favorite paintings.

Top right: "Picasso Lips," another painting by Nick.

Bottom: One of Nick's hand-painted snare drums.

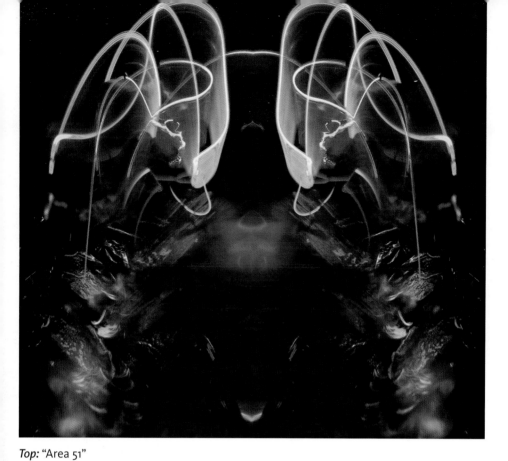

Top: "Area 51"

Bottom: "Influx"

Two of Nick's popular SceneFour laser drum-art-pieces.

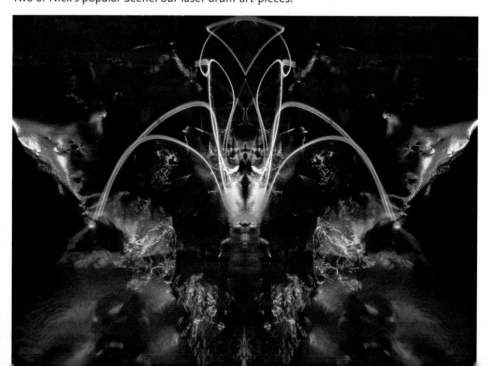

Top: Nick performs with Steve Lukather, Gilby Clarke, Marky Ramone, Jogen Carlsson, and others at the 95.5 KLOS/Whisky A Go Go's Rock Against MS All Star benefit concert on October 17, 2013.

Bottom: The last photo ever taken of Nick's drum set on stage at the Baked Potato, May 21, 2016.

TATTOO YOU

We were doing an in-store promotion of one of our new albums, meeting fans and signing autographs when this young dude came up and asked Dave and me to sign his arm.

I was like, "Sure, bro," and wrote a big "X." Dave took his black marker and drew a squiggly line up the kid's arm.

After the show that night, we saw the same dude. He'd managed to get an after-show pass and came up to us.

"Yo, dudes, check it out! I got your signatures tattooed on my arm!"

Dave and I just looked at each other.

"Come on!" I said. "We would have signed our names if you'd told us you were going to do that!"

The kid didn't care. "It's cool, bro! I know who did it! I know who wrote it!"

That was fucked up. Poor bastard has an "X" and a squiggly line tattooed on his arm, and he's going around saying, "Yeah, these are the guys from Megadeth's signatures!"

Fuck poor penmanship; they can't even write their own names!

CHAPTER FIVE

IN MY LIFE

Forget *Breaking Bad*, I got a great idea for a killer new drama on AMC— *The Walking Meth*. It's about a whole generation of dudes stumbling around, gaunt with ghost-white skin, looking like they died sometime last year. Probably smelling that way, too.

I know all about it because I *was* one for a short time.

Those sex, drugs and rock 'n' roll fairytales are mostly true, but that shit ain't glamorous. Read a memoir by just about any of my peers, or watch *Decline of Western Civilization: The Metal Years*, and then tell me any of that shit's a good idea. Yeah, buckle down, 'cause I'm going to lecture.

Drugs weren't my thing during the Megadeth days, and I never went on stage messed up. Ever. I don't care what anybody says; you can't get up there and do a good job playing drums in a metal band—well, any band—if you're fucked up. Look at some of the YouTube footage of me playing with Megadeth: there's no way anyone can get up on stage wasted and put in a performance like I did, night after night for ten years. That's marathon, endurance drumming, dude.

And opiates? Hate them. Nobody should fuck with dope. I've never seen that end well—ever, for anyone. We lose way too many beautiful, talented, and sensitive people to heroin. They either overdose ,or their spirits wither and die as they continue to zombie around in broken shells of bodies. I didn't like the people who were associated with it and never liked to be around the people I loved who were using. It's an evil fucking drug. Heinous. No one is exempt from that shit. I tried pretty much every drug, and heroin was the one I hated the most. Early on in my time in the band, the two Daves would lay out rails of smack in the control rooms or on the amps and offer everyone around a straw. I did it once. That's the absolute truth. Every other time, I waited for them and then put the straw up to my nose and blew out. By then they were so torqued that they never noticed what I'd done, except to think that I was balls-deep in the party just like them. I wasn't.

That shit never did anyone in Megadeth any good. Mustaine fucked himself up bad. So did Junior, and it cost us millions of dollars in cancelled tours, commitments, and responsibilities. Both of them wrote about it in their own books. And now here I am to tell you that while at the end my attitude was pretty shitty and I didn't even try to get along with Mustaine, I never fucked off a show.

Juan Alvarez:
I'll be one of a hundred people to tell you that Nick was never into hard drugs during Megadeth. I was there. It's hands down total bullshit that Mustaine says he was doing drugs while he was in Megadeth. It's impossible; no fucking way someone could fill their lungs with that shit and go out and play like Nick did every night. The drugs didn't start until after Mustaine fired Nick.

After we went to Europe in 1989 supporting Iron Maiden and played Castle Donington, Junior's heroin addiction leveled him. As slippery as they can sometimes be, Junior grabbed onto the reins of sobriety and held on tight. He went through a hellish year of relapses and rehabs, but he made it through the storm. For him, he's said, the urge to not do drugs became more powerful than the desire to do drugs. Very cool. Every clean and sober dude has a basket full of sayings and clichés that are fucking annoying when you're drinking and using, but when you're not, you realize that they're clichés because they're true. When you're living them instead of living dirty, surprise, surprise, you're not fucked up anymore. It's one of the things that's made me decide to be completely forthright about my own struggles.

Drugs, as Junior put it, "can make you feel unique, (but) completely takes away our uniqueness. We're like any other junkie. Using alcohol and drugs is an equalizer. We just blend in. So, the best part of us goes away."

It's been sad that this hasn't come so easily for Mustaine, who at last count has gone through sixteen or seventeen rehabs, and now in 2016 has a winery and a beer company and Tweets about having to blow off an autograph session with fans because he'd been too loaded the night before on some heinous Italian liquor. I'm not trying to be a dick and throw stones, but dude, when you make a big deal out of being clean and sober I believe you have a responsibility to the fans and people who look up to you to be righteous.

"Some (sober) people can never drink like normal people, but I can and I do," he says. "David (Ellefson) is sober, I drink when I want to."

Well, God bless, dude. Just please, mercy, don't sit in with the San Diego Symphony—any symphony—ever, ever again. There might be children or perfect pitch people in the audience, and remember, they probably haven't had as much grape juice as you have. (Ok, that was probably mean, but when I saw footage of him doing that, I reached for my phone and nearly dialed to say, "*Dude!* Fuck! Don't *do* that!" Sort of like you'd try to talk a suicide jumper off the ledge.)

My first few years in the band had their moments, but everyone was pretty healthy and focused. We were on the road with *Countdown To Extinction* for most of 1992, and in January the following year we got another Grammy nomination and booked an American tour with Stone Temple Pilots opening for us. That was the beginning of what would be a long, brutal decline.

I was so saddened to learn of Scott Weiland's death. Tragic. The last time I saw him, he came over to my place with my old bandmate Anthony

Before

Gallo. The two of them were clean and sober, but Scott had about twenty grand in his pocket. It turned into a blaze of strip clubs, drugs, and booze that wiped us all out for a few days. And, no, it wasn't a good idea even at the time. Drugs are deadly and they *suck*.

Megadeth and STP were booked for a tour of Japan and then Australia after our American tour followed by a tour supporting Aerosmith later that summer. Everything went south when Mustaine overdosed in Eugene, Oregon in February. The whole band ground to a halt and all the shows were cancelled for the next six months as he went off to rehab again. We were all upset, not as much at Dave but certainly for him. It sucks to see anyone you care about in such a death spiral, but he really let us all down on that one. Part of Dave's struggle is denial, and he ended up kind of turning the tables on us and making his problems ours. He'd played on Diamond Head's *Death and Progress* album, and we were invited to play with them and Metallica on their European tour, which was enormously cool. One slight catch: Mustaine insisted that if he had to be clean and sober, so did we. I totally respect his desire for sobriety and never drinking, or being under the influence, around him—but, dude, this is *your* problem, not mine.

This was the first time Megadeth was to perform with Metallica, the bane of Mustaine's existence since they'd fired him for substance abuse back in the day. Whether it was privately or publicly, Dave was never far from railing on about Lars or James or Kirk, whom he hated for taking his gig. After Dave fired me, I've always felt like saying to him, "Dude, it must have really sucked when they fired you from your band, eh?"

I'm not saying I was an angel. I had a blast out on the road. I liked to get a little high, and I loved a few beers after a show. I never had a problem with what Mustaine did or didn't do. It was none of my business unless it affected us or seriously compromised his health. And when it didn't, hey, cool. On that tour, however, Mustaine decided that everyone had to abstain from all drugs and alcohol. He told us that everyone on the road was going to have to take urine analysis tests and sign a binding contract so that he could know everyone in the band and crew was sober. I was like, fuck that, I'm not peeing in a cup. No way. I was so not into it. You're going to question whether I'm doing my job or not by making me pee in a cup? Can't do it. Sorry. It's such an infringement on my private business. If I begin to blow it when it comes to doing my job, of course, hold me accountable. But if I'm cool, what's wrong with having a few beers after a show? I wasn't the dude fucking up shows, causing them to be cancelled because I couldn't stand up or know what song I was playing.

Neither was Marty, or, by this time, Junior. The sound dude never had to dial me or any of us back in the mix because we were playing a different song than the rest of the band. And, yes, there were times Mustaine was dialed way back by the sound guys because the shows would have sucked even more than they did. That happened before I was the drummer and happened more than I care to remember once I was the drummer. We were a band, and we had to look out for each other and the best interests of Megadeth itself. But, for me, that did not include absolutely everything that Dave got into his head. It was great whenever he cleaned up and tried valiantly to stay sober on the road. Everyone respected that. But, like I said earlier, I'm not peeing in a cup for anyone.

Some of our "group" sessions were cool. Some of them were lame and made everybody uncomfortable, like the band AA meetings, and the prayer meetings. At one point, Dave, who's a black belt in some martial art, brought Sensei Benny the Jet Urquidez on tour for our workouts (at great expense). He was awesome, I admit. Sometimes he'd make Dave jog behind the bus. After a while, though, we were like, "Dude, we just want to get to the next city and get into the hotel."

For Dave, it wasn't a fad; he was really into it. I admire anyone who gets into those kinds of routines to better himself. Fuck knows I was humbled, because no way was I ever capable of those kinds of workouts! Besides, I got mine every night on the drum riser. And on "non-performance days" I'd get it mountain biking. Sensei Benny's sessions were lethal. I tried the kickboxing a few times but was just destroyed afterward. He'd say, "That wasn't the workout, that was the warmup! *Now* we work out!" I'd start whining like a little girl, "Sensei, I have to play tonight!"

It was hardcore, but that's Dave. Hardcore healthy or hardcore strung out. He really didn't like it when there were people around him who could have a few beers or smoke a joint and not end up in rehab a week later, their hair terminally fucked up, teeth and skin yellow, nose bleeding and track marks like a bad case of chicken pox. I'm not pretending I didn't partake in the whole scene for the ten years I was out there. If there's a Spinal Tap notch in my belt, (*Mom, don't read this part*) it's probably from when all four chicks in Drain got me destroyed on Jäger-meister, and I did all four of them. There's the obligatory sex-on-the-road story for you.

(Ok, Mom, come on back.)

We always had to come up with aliases when we went out on the road or were in another city recording or doing publicity or videos or whatever. It's for security, for our own egos, (let's be honest) and it's for fun. It's always a contest to see who comes up with the best names. My choice hotel names were, in no particular order: Luscious Balls, Sport Wood, and, my favorite, Justin Sider. (Oh, shit, sorry Mom. It's ok now. Really.)

I was never a big drinker, but I liked a cold beer after a show or some whacky concoction in a coconut shell out at the pool in the summer. I'm Italian, so wine's cool with me. But getting wasted isn't having a good time, at least for me. That shit gets old. Sure, I wish it had have gotten old for me a long time before it did, but everything happens for a reason. I've always liked to smoke pot to relax and chill out and watch cartoons, but drugs turned out to be a fucking heinous curse in my life for a few years after Mustaine fired me. That's when I got myself into trouble with speed. I don't think I have an addictive personality, but getting fired slayed me. It's the only time in my life I was seriously depressed. I didn't want to do anything, go anywhere, see anyone, or be anyone. And I got really sick. I can't downplay it and I'm not going to.

Donia Menza:
I know absolutely 100 percent for sure he was never into that shit when he was in Megadeth. It was Mustaine firing Nick that led him to doing hard drugs. It was such a letdown and such a state of depression that he didn't know what to do. Then some asshole came to the house and said, "Try this." That was it. He immediately became distant. Nick used to call me all the time. Now, he wouldn't answer the door or come over. He got really anti-social. He was losing weight; his skin and hair changed. We witnessed it. I finally came clean with my mom and dad. Dad went over and told him how worried we were. From that day on, Nick became part of the family again. He'd taken a wrong path, but he turned the corner.

At first, I was so vain that I didn't want to get to the point where I was at rock bottom and always told myself, and my friends, that I could quit when I wanted. When I had something better to do. That's one of the

After

first evil things about The Big Lie of Drugs. Once it's got you, it's too late. There were whole years where I didn't look in the mirror. I didn't leave the house. There was tinfoil on the windows and garbage everywhere. I lived between the studio and the bathroom, except on the rare occasions I'd pass through the kitchen on my way upstairs. I didn't let anyone see me because I knew they'd say, "Oh, he's fucked up on drugs."

Finally, I couldn't help it. No drug addict can. Smoking meth takes a toll unlike any other drug. Meth fucked me up and nearly took me out. With YouTube and the internet and everything, being a dude in front of the cameras and being interviewed and all that, I couldn't hide. I can't hide it now. I look like a corpse in some of those videos. It's hideous. When I see or listen to interviews I did back then, in the mid-2000s or so, it's awful. Believe me, all you fans out there who care, I pay attention to what people say, no matter how hard it is to hear.

When I saw, over the years, the comments on a few videos, it really hit hard, because there was no way I could deny what I was doing to myself. Some of those (unedited) comments have stayed with me:

NICK MAN! STOP DOING THAT SHIT :(can't you see there are thousands of ppl that love you n love your playing?!!! we need you healthy stupid ass!!! cmon!!!

It's very sad to see a great drummer like nick, playing in a small band. He looks sick, i'm very sad now

Man Nick is also a fellow July 23 Leo, and damn it is hard to see him like this! Come on Nick bring that Lion spirit back!

what a waste.

aww nick :(you look so sad . . . he was so cute and lively before ;_; It's never too late, clean yourself up and go back to Megadeth ^-^ You're a fucking awesome drummer :D

omg what happened to nick??? he seems totally drained and lacking energy. hope he gets back to full health soon! :-)

wow doesn't even look like him anymore omg he looks horrible

nick is in bad shape

nick i feel really bad for you it seems that you have been going through depression since you got kicked out and you look SOOOOOOO different your really pale and your getting really boney

Man, I wish Nick would get off the drugs & get his shit together. If he would, we'd have back 3/4 of the RIP lineup back, because Mustaine said if Nick would clean up, he'd let him back in the band. But most importantly, Nick would be healthy again...

You never see Nick smile anymore :(

The real sad part is that He's been on Drugs, He's been through hell with it and now he's beating it by standing here today. And you guys Are saying he looks like shit and he's fucked up, Like C'mon! Good to see him moving forward and stuff, Why don't you support the guy Menza is like one of the coolest drummers on earth (my opinion).

Nick is completely fucked up.

The reality of that shit stung. It made me feel even worse. Can you imagine complete strangers writing this about you? At first, it made me sink lower, feeling like I was letting everybody down. There I was at one point with millions in the bank, two amazing boys, a great talent for which I was known all over the world, and the most awesome mom and dad and sister ever—and it was all ending up a brown stain on the bottom of a glass pipe.

It took me a long time to figure this out, but here's what happened. Nobody who's coming up in the world and is truly doing well in his profession or dream is on drugs. Simple. The happiest day for me was when I figured that out and realized I could step away from it. I didn't need that shit. It was fucking me up. It was spiritually, mentally, and emotionally bogging me down in a dark place of negative energy that made me inferior, lazy, crazy, and pissed off. I realized how blessed I am to have so many thousands of people who care about me, and hated seeing me that way—and had the balls to post exactly how they felt, that they hoped I'd get straight. Now *that* is awesome, dude! That was empowering. Not at first, but ultimately it was. So, if you're one of those people, thank you! You helped me. You really did.

So did Mustaine, surprisingly, with something he wrote about himself and addiction: "At some point you have to take ownership of the things people are saying about you."

No matter what else, at the end of the day Mustaine is one smart dude. Maybe that gets him in trouble and makes him a difficult dude to work with sometimes, but he's totally right. From there on I made the best choice.

I've given it all up for the best stuff in the universe that's fucking us all up: oil and grease and sugar and salt! Bring it on. I actually recently tried to kick sugar, and that ain't happening, dude. I need my Jolly Ranchers. There's no way Dr. Drew or Betty Ford or anyone else is going to get in my way.

Now, for me, my kids being around, I'm trying to go back down the same avenues and come out at the same creative places (but without the drugs) and see if I can see anything that was left out when I was high. I don't know the route; I'm just not willing to put myself in jeopardy by using drugs again to get to that place. A lot of people will tell you "I used drugs because I was depressed; I was fucked up; my life was going nowhere and my wife divorced me and my mom died and I got in a car wreck." I ran to drugs when I didn't have the emotional strength to deal with the devastation of what Mustaine had done to me. Life was too painful. I didn't know how to ask for help, and I have the best upbringing and family ever.

Of course, they stepped in when it got so bad that my denials didn't cut it any more. I call my mom and dad and Donia the world's "Most Functional Family in History." I can't even think what it must be like for people who don't have great families and friends. For me, it was too many years I can't get back. But I can make sure I don't lose any more time.

I meditate now. In my own way, I continue to pray. I never ask for specific things. I just ask for balance.

The real Nick is cool. He's a goof sometimes, but I like him.

Dude, if you take drugs and they're not being administered by a doctor, you'll probably end up dying. If you are taking addictive drugs prescribed by a doctor and you don't really need them, you're putting yourself at risk. I wish I'd been able to avoid drugs, but I am resigned that there really wasn't much of a chance of that. I wish I'd gotten out at the age of twenty-five, like Junior. I never wanted to talk about my experiences, but if even one dude never picks up a pipe because of my story, my pain was worth it.

I think everybody has voices in their heads—the voice of reason, the voice of your heart, the voice of the outside ideas that come in from the universe or god or wherever.

I partied hard with the worst of them. I know where that place is and I don't need to go back there because it's a one-dimensional place. It's suppressing. A weight gets put on you that you don't need to carry around.

I don't function well under the influence like that. It's not my thing. There's a lot of bad energy and bad people that go with it. I don't do negative, and I don't do drama. There's so much negative in the world with everything we do. Why do you need to go and enhance that by doing drugs?

It got to the point where I was, like, "Oh, let's go and get an eight-ball and smoke it all at once." Then you're bummed because nothing's going on, and you don't have any money and your account is overdrawn. You're depressed about everything, and then you've given yourself something *else* to be depressed about. Fuck that shit.

I used to struggle, along with my kids' mom, Terri. How young do we tell the boys about drugs? Of course, they're gonna say, "We're never going to do drugs, Dad!" You can't tell them too young, or they're likely to get curious: "I wonder what this does? Why do other people take this? Let's try it and see what happens." But you want to alert them to the stop signs. There's no playbook for having children, and like adults, every kid is different. My boys are pretty much perfection. They're a handful, believe me, and I love them even more for it! But they also couldn't be more unlike each other. They're advanced for their ages. I'm just trying to inform them and prepare them the best I can; advise them about what's right and what is wrong, especially drugs.

A few years into our great rise and fall together, Junior, Marty, and the crew and I developed a way to tell how things were going to be that week or that month. When Mustaine was in a white shirt, like a dress shirt, all pressed and like a gentleman, we knew he was straight. If he was wearing a black t-shirt or cut-up shirt, that's when we knew he was fucked up, and we were in for a bad night.

When the video for our cover of Alice Cooper's "No More Mister Nice Guy" was shot by director Penelope Spheeris, Mustaine showed up to the gig "so fried on heroin and other drugs that he could not sing and play guitar at the same time; therefore, the singing and playing had to be recorded separately," she later recalled.

Nowadays, I have a list of which rock stars deserve a smack in the mouth. John Bonham for fuckin' dying! Keith Moon, Hendrix, Morrison, Janis, Scott Weiland, Layne, and then Mike Starr from Alice In Chains; Cobain, Amy Winehouse—seriously, any of the dozens and dozens of greats who died, and are joined by men and women (kids, really, a lot of them) snuffed out on the losing end of drugs and alcohol. How dare they take their awesome talents and beings away from the world.

I've never met a happy junkie. Come to think of it, I've never met a happy choreographer, either, but you get the idea.

All this tired, cliché behavior on the road is pretty predictable. Or was, for the most part. These days, touring is how bands and record companies, make money, so it's all business now. The party's over. You can't just fuck up hotel rooms and private jets and dressing rooms anymore and expect to have a career. The accountants and executives run the biz now with an iron fist that they only dreamed of ten or fifteen years ago.

Gone are the "fun" days of legendary rock 'n' roll road stories: Nikki Sixx repeatedly overdosing and being left in a dumpster in London by his drug dealer; Zeppelin using a shark as a dildo at the Edgewater hotel in Seattle, where people could fish right out of the windows; Keith Moon destroying so many hotel rooms that the incidents "tend to blend together into one big ball of devastation." I read somewhere that one such rampage cost Moon about a half a million bucks. Yeah, that's fun, right?

I'll tell ya firsthand that it's not. I didn't destroy an entire floor at the Riot House or drive anything but my bicycle into the pool. (Did you know it's illegal to ride a bicycle in a swimming pool in California? It's true. It's actually on the books, along with the statute that you can be fined for using skivvies to wash your car. But I digress.)

I do have the requisite rock 'n' roll trashed-hotel-room story. Just one. We were in New Orleans, and I was at this cool old hotel in the French Quarter with awesome antique furniture and ankle-deep carpets that you'd hate to drop a lit joint into. The TV was in one of those entertainment units with big, heavy doors, and I was reaching down to pick up the remote, which I'd dropped. I came up and hit my head on the corner of the door. I'm like, "motherfuckingsonofabitchmotherfucker!!" I took the remote and slammed it into the TV, breaking it. "Wow, that felt really good!" There was a lamp there with one of those boom arms, so I took that and swung it into the wall. Then I broke the phone and the table lamp, and a couple seconds later there's this knock.

"Is everything all right in there, sir?"

"Everything's fine."

"Can we talk to you?"

"Yep."

I opened the door, handed the guy my Visa card and said, "This will pay for the damages."

He looked in and saw I'd fucking destroyed the room. I don't know; it felt right. And once I started doing it, it felt like exactly the thing to do. It wasn't, of course. It was really fucked up. I don't know why I got so enraged like that. It cost me about five grand. The hotel manager came in afterwards to give me my credit card back. He looked around as I stood there, kind of embarrassed.

"I've always wanted to throw a TV out the window!" he said.

I said, "Go for it, dude, it's paid for!"

My Mom was like, "What's this bill here for five thousand dollars?!"

"Oh, I had a little accident in my room and broke some stuff."

"Nick! You're not on drugs, are you?"

"No, Mom, I had a few beers, but..."

We really didn't get into a whole lot of that kind of behavior. It's too expensive, and I don't think many of us were interested in the unwelcome attention of hotel security (or worse).

The two Daves, Marty and I, and a bunch of our crew were in the pool at the hotel in Rio one afternoon, however, and we all got to witness a spectacular display of room destruction by Axl Rose. After having seen one of our opening acts using his "exclusive" ramps on the main stage, he blew a fuse, throwing his television, phone, and all kinds of shit out the window into the pool near us, a dozen or so stories below.

Thankfully, he didn't hit or injure anyone. If there's any welcome behavior modification with the maturing of rock 'n' roll and how it's become so corporate and concerned about the bottom line, it's that just about everybody out there is clean and sober, and there isn't a record company or tour sponsor on the planet who will put up with the antics of yesteryear. Tours are way too lucrative to cancel in an age where albums are no longer the primary source of profits, and there are way too many attorneys hiding out between the clauses in contracts.

My transgression in N'awlins cured me of that kind of acting out. Once before, early on, I'd broken a porcelain sink in a dressing room by tossing a chair when I'd come off stage furious at myself for not having played well. I immediately felt bad, and the band's wardrobe magician, Dawn Brumley, who is the most awesome sweetheart ever, helped me find the manager of the venue so I could pay for the damage I'd caused. I did steal a showerhead once from a hotel room in Argentina. It was this monster the size of my snare that pumped out a wicked spray. It went into one of my road cases and eventually found its way onto one of my showers at home. Best ever, dude!

Strippers and porn stars and whatever on the road? What do you think? It's a heavy metal rock band. But Megadeth—actually every band I've been in—was not big into groupies (certainly not in the way of our legendary road-warrior forefathers).

Sure, we had our entourage of girls backstage and at the hotels, but, honestly, I didn't go out of my way to fuck any of my fans. I was super-selective. I'm not boasting. Megadeth was not into degrading our fans. We appreciated them; they're the reason we were there. I think it's important to be cool to the fans. You shouldn't be a dick to the people who put you there. That's my philosophy about the whole grand scheme of things: it's supposed to be fun. The drama and everything about taking yourself too seriously are the things that drag the whole business down. Like all the fake "worship the devil" shit in heavy metal. I mean, it's dope on that cartoon sort of level when you're twenty, but it's so old, man. Artists who have any growth in them at all have some responsibility to at least think about what they're doing and who the audience is. I mean, kids find that sinister, violent, death-and-hell-in-the-title stuff interesting and cool.

I was into it when I was a teenager. Skulls and fire and all that shit. But when you grow up and you're out there seriously doing music, it's like really, are you going to go there? Are you going to base your whole existence on that? As you get older, you realize it would be cool to have all the heaviness and the toughness without all that silly imagery going on.

I think violent stuff is terribly desensitizing, so when some kids (the total minority, mind you) get into that type of behavior it's no big deal to them because they've already been desensitized by video games or movies. People generally don't just come up with radical and danger-ous ideas out of the air. Well, of course, some people do. But not sinister, sinister shit. When you see something like that in a movie you're like, "I can't believe that happened. I can't believe somebody thought of that," but it makes you think about it. If you've never been exposed to that type of shit, then you probably wouldn't have those type of thoughts unless you're a truly evil person. Like I said, I just try to advise my kids about what's right and what is wrong.

I've always kept this in mind. And the more I see, the more I experi-ence, the wiser I am about what I do, what I say, and what I put out there. For instance, it's a small thing but important to me, I don't put the words death or die in a title any more. When you put anything that ugly, it cuts out an entire audience of people.

I've been doing music long enough to know what's going to get looked at and what's not. If you don't want anyone to look at your shit and don't care, then write songs about the devil and dying and killing, anything negative and ugly.

How tired does Rage Against the Machine get, where every one of their songs is anti-government, or anti-something? Cool dudes who can really play but, man, I've heard it, *ok*? Total negative energy. There's a market for that stuff—kids who think it's tough—but it's only going to get you so far.

I love Slayer and nearly joined the band, but they're totally deviled out. Not for real, but their image is. After ten or twenty years, it's all passé shit; it's all been done and used and overused again and again. I'm not saying don't get into those topics. We need those topics. We need to write about them, and sing about them and see them in movies and stuff; but it could all use a little intelligence.

I also think we need more music and writing based on truth and real life instead of comic book fantasy. I'm probably not explaining myself very well, but here's a great example from my life. When my grandmother died, it was heartbreaking. There's just no feeling as bleak and hopelessly empty as losing a family member. I hate to say it, but I've always wanted to die before my mom and dad because I don't think

I could survive going through their deaths. After my grandmother's service, my mom came to me and said, "When I looked at your grandmother at the funeral, I wondered if she could hear me call her name. I wondered if she knew I was there."

My mom, who had never written a song or a poem or lyric or anything in her life, that I know of, wrote a thing she called, "When I Die Will I Find You There?"

When I looked at it, I was like, "Those are cool lyrics!"

She had all these great lines, and I had music already. I never write music to lyrics; I match lyrics up to music that's done. I tried to fit them into something I thought was perfect for what she'd written, and I think it came out pretty good. When I recorded it and put it on my first solo record, I re-titled it "In My Life."

In my life, there used to be drugs and downward spirals, blowing every opportunity and good thing to come along. No more. In my life now is the promise of every day, without drugs and destruction and negativity. I hope you have that in your life.

RANDOM ACTS OF DANGER

I went skydiving. Once. That'll never happen again.

I like doing stupid shit on my mountain bike, and I like dogsleds and snowmobiles in Alaska and whatever. But stepping out of a perfectly good airplane with what looks like an oversized hoodie is not my idea of a good time.

Mustaine was into it in the early '90s when he was trying to swap one dangerous rush for another. We had a song on the *Countdown* album called "High Speed Dirt" that gets its title from the buzzword for what a skydiver experiences when his chute doesn't deploy. Sort of like Icarus in reverse: he didn't fly too close to the sun; he flew too close to the ground!

Junior and I went along with the program and did a tandem jump, screaming all the way down. Marty refused. He said he'd do it if the album went platinum, a pledge he had to fulfill when the record went double platinum. When he did finally jump, he excitedly said he loved the experience but would never do it again. I hated the experience and will never do it again. Well, hating is not exactly true. When I was floating after the chute came out, it was awesome—really peaceful and quiet. You can hear what's going on below on the ground, which surprised me, but I'm not doing it ever again. Once was enough.

I'm not about to go surfing again, either, which sucks because I used to love surfing at Zuma beach in Malibu. I thought I was pretty good, too, and I took the dirty lickings with the epic rides and enjoyed everything about it. Then one day I ate it on a big wave, and things went wrong in an instant. The wave dragged me under, and I instinctively swam for the surface. No panic; I knew what I was doing. So I thought. With one of my strokes, my outreached hand touched sand: I had swum in the wrong direction, hitting the ocean floor. I wasn't that deep, but I was out of air and panicked. It really fucked me up. That was it for surfing.

Before I truly learned that lesson, however, I got into some cliff diving in Hawaii—a hobby that went wrong quickly when I dove into a coral reef and was immediately getting pounded by waves. I was unable to swim out of it. Before I got all cut up or in serious trouble, I was able to grab onto the back of a big tortoise that swam me away from the rocks.

That was it for cliff diving.

I love snorkeling, and I'll keep doing that. But, of course, I thought I'd dial it up and get my scuba certification, also on a trip to Hawaii. I took all the classes and got out there and really got into it, but the instructor said I wasn't compliant with all the rules and kept giving me shit. I am too easily distracted by what I see and what really turns me on, and I'd use up all my air in thirty minutes just staying in one place against the current if there was something I was checking out—or, like the last time I was scuba diving and failed the course, I just got myself lost in all the amazing fish and coral. It's another world down there. I had some beef jerky that I was feeding the fish, but then I got kind of concerned that it might attract some larger species I wasn't so interested in meeting. I went to the bottom to collect some shells and saw this huge blue abalone-looking one. I went to grab it, and it turned out to be this massive blue crab that raised up to attack me. I went for the surface like a rocket. When I broke through the surface I saw that I had drifted a long way from the boat. There were no buddy divers around me. (Or I wasn't around my buddy divers, I guess is more the truth.) For the instructor, that was Strike Three. Probably for the best. You can die in the ocean quickly when you're just out there trying to have fun.

That was it for scuba diving.

I was with my boys in Alaska on an awesome vacation, and we were all-in with every winter activity we could do. It's one of our best trips yet together. But, of course, I got myself a little too close to random danger. Snowmobiling is awesome, right up until you slam into a wall of snow and go in like fifteen feet, getting buried. It didn't happen to me, but it happened to one of the dudes out with us one day. We'd been taught that if you get covered by an avalanche (or by riding your machine into a mountain of snow) it'll be pitch-black; you'll panic and start flailing about. You'll freak and begin hyperventilating. We were taught to lie down and roll, roll, and roll and you'll make it out of the pack if you're relaxed, stay calm, and take short breaths of air. Cool, eh?

Nobody got hurt when we were out, but it was a little freaky. We'll still go out, but we're a little more aware of the dangers.

Also in Alaska on that trip, I decided that it was just too much temptation to not go dogsledding. It's Alaska, right? I signed right up. They gave me a flare gun and taught me how to fire it. I signed all these waivers that cheerily certified that if I stayed out after dark I'd die, and that they weren't responsible—that if I fell off and got tangled up I could die, and they weren't responsible. There were a lot of forms telling me all the ways I could die, for which they wouldn't be responsible. I was stoked! And it was one of the most amazing experiences of my life. I'd do that again in a heartbeat.

For the most part these days, I keep my random acts of danger on two wheels, off-road. For a long time now mountain biking has been my main source of recreation. It helped get me clean and healthy, and nowadays it's like its own kind of drug for me. I go up into the hills above Ventura Boulevard and come screaming down the paths; it's exhilarating and it's always the great payoff for the workout of biking up. I'm not doing some of the jumps and stunts I once did. I'm serious about keeping myself with the wheels down! Recently, though, I did have a remarkable close encounter. I was hauling ass down this hill above Laurel when I came around a corner and surprised a coyote mother and her pups. Usually they'll clear out of a human's way long before you even see them, but I was going too fast, and they didn't have a chance. Instead, she attacked me. I'm proud I didn't fall, but she did manage to gnarl on my bike a bit. And she bit my ass. I have bragging rights because I didn't lose it, and I have a cool road story to tell.

CHAPTER SIX

"WILL THE REAL NICK MENZA PLEASE SIT DOWN?"

When Dave Mustaine fired me from my dream job there was only one thing I knew for sure: I didn't want to join another band and go back out on the road.

I was absolutely crushed. It wasn't an emotional rollercoaster, it was a fucking cluster of terror-inducing bungee plunges, and if you've ever bungee jumped, you know that even if you're lucky enough to not flatten your forehead into the ground, you don't rebound all the way back up to where you began. There's no going back to the beginning. That's what happened to me within the space of a few weeks after I was diagnosed with the tumor in my knee. There was the positive and relieving outcome of the surgery and then my dismissal from Megadeth. I felt as if I'd never bounce back. I didn't want to do anything. I didn't leave my house for six months, unless it was to go to my Mom and Dad's. I didn't want to see friends, and I was terrified of what I thought would be the shame of seeing fans or reporters.

For the decade I was with the band, I'd never been home for more than two or three weeks at a time, adding to the whirlwind and extremes of my rock-star life. This is not me bitching. It's all just a part of the life that you don't think about or even consider when you get swept away when you're young and in a huge band. I understood when Joe Walsh sang, "I have a mansion, but forget the price. Ain't never been there; they tell me it's nice."

We would do three hundred shows a year. I wouldn't unpack my suitcase when I was back at the house. Why bother? I'd come home for, like, a week, and I'd leave my suitcase at the front door with the lid open and just take what I need out of it and put stuff back into it, 'cause I knew I was gonna close it up in four or five days. That was the suckiest part about touring—every time you'd get home, the clock would quickly start ticking out the time before you left again.

It seemed that I didn't live in my house for the first five years after buying it. I bought it in 1995 when we were touring extensively. We'd come home for Christmas and maybe two days at Thanksgiving. It ruined my time at the house because it never felt like home. I couldn't do anything to relax and unwind because I knew that I'd have to go right back out. I never did stop living out of suitcases and tour bags. But I guess that's the life, isn't it? It's either all *on*, all the time, or all *off*.

After about fifteen years of bands, writing, recording, and touring the world and never truly settling down with anyone anywhere, I was suddenly at a polar opposite. I felt that I had nowhere to go, nothing to do, and no one I wanted to do it with.

I was so miserable and angry I didn't play drums or listen to music. I wanted to sue Mustaine; plead, beg, anything to make me feel like I had some control over my life and career. I simply didn't have the energy. It took me months of moping around before I was actually rested. Then I was overcome with this great feeling of being grounded, just this sense of stability that I'd never had before. It was like, "Wow! I don't have to go anywhere, call anyone, or do anything."

I have a lot of friends, and my phone rang constantly. It seemed like hundreds of them called, all great people who wished me well and didn't want anything from me. Then there were a lot more calls from people who weren't so selfless.

The first job offer was from Wasp, who were looking for a drummer as soon as I got fired from Megadeth. I turned them down over the phone. No disrespect, but my heart wasn't in joining another metal band after having spent most of my career in the best one on the planet. I was getting a lot of calls from heavy metals bands, which is understandable. That's what I'm known for. It just wasn't motivating for me.

It honestly took me about three years to reprogram myself. It was like post-traumatic stress disorder. Everybody's kind of standing still from your normal routine where you're moving every day to a different place, different city; different people. If there's anything good about it, it's the boost to your immune system.

Seriously—if you take care of yourself on the road, and you're not drunk or high all the time, you can be ready to take on all the germs, different environments, and the dirtiest thing of all: people. I'd always do meet-and-greets and shake people's hands, and I'd leave my gloves on. People would be like, "Dude, how come you're wearing gloves?" And I'm like, "It's not to protect me from you; it's to protect you from me." People are standing in line picking their noses and biting their nails, not washing their hands after going to the bathroom—when you're in a line meeting a hundred kids every night, you become a walking hazmat experiment if you're not careful.

I got sick whenever I got home too. I think that when you're putting your body through the rigor of the road and suddenly stop, your body and mind go into shock. You're not living your life on a schedule any more.

After the first years of doing absolutely nothing—and I mean, nothing, dude—I slowly started to come out of it and began to think about music again. I probably had hundreds of songs and song ideas from all my years out on the road, because as I said I didn't go out of my room all that much once I'd already seen whatever there was to see in whichever city. I'd sit in my room and paint or draw or play guitar and write. I had fully intended on contributing songs to the band, but Mustaine hated anybody else writing songs. He didn't mind us coming up with ideas, but he didn't want us coming up with stuff that he couldn't take credit for. Besides, Dave always has so many good ideas himself.

It was never the collaboration the rest of us wanted it to be. It was difficult, like pulling teeth, to write songs in that band. I kept bringing songs in, and he was, like, "Nah, you just stick to playing drums, and let me worry about the songwriting."

I was depressed, and I tried to get myself through it by making a solo record. That became *Life After Deth*. You write what you know about. All the songs are about Megadeth and my time in the band. (All my songs are about things that happen to me. I don't write about drugs or sex or stupid shit. I write about a lot of things that are just going on in my environment or my mind.)

Writing music is a very personal thing, and it comes out of places deep in your brain, in your heart, or in your soul. It's not a shared experience until the songs come out and you've written them down and start recording them—unless they're songs that you're writing with other people and you have a shared experience; like being in the same band, being out on the road, and being together. These were songs I had to do myself. The music is stuff that I was writing during my career with Megadeth. It was like Megadeth meets Dream Theatre with a touch of White Zombie. I did this to get stuff off my chest. Like my paintings, it was an experimental art thing. Some of the music was from before I joined Megadeth and a snapshot of the times. At first, I wasn't even sure I would make it public. It was more of a personal thing, a project to kill some time and try to get an idea of what I wanted to do and where I wanted to go.

I did it at my studio over the course of a couple of years. I play the drums, the bass, the guitars and do all the main vocals. I had some help, of course—Anthony Gallo's a guitarist from Venice and the whole Suicidal Tendencies/Los Cycos crowd who's been around playing in all kinds of bands for years. He had a cool band called Jesus Chrysler at one point (great name, eh?). He and I jammed a lot and put together the first real band I was in after Megadeth, which we called Chodle's Trunk. There was this guy around in the neighborhood called Chodle who ran with the dangerous White Fence gang, and if you ended up in Chodle's trunk, it meant you were going to be taken down to the railroad tracks and have the shit beaten out of you. If you were lucky.

We did a record, but all we got offered was a Japanese deal for like ten grand. We thought, *Wow. We spent more recording it.* That died on the vine as I moved onto the solo record. It was the mark of me starting to come back. Bassist Jason Levin, who'd been playing in the Venice band Radio I-Ching, came in, and Christian Nesmith, the son of Monkees founder Michael Nesmith, did some leads. Anthony Peter Biuso helped out on a song, and Max Norman co-produced with me.

Christian Nesmith:
Nick was working on that material for a few years before he was fired from Megadeth. He'd come over to my place and hang out, or I'd go over there. Sometimes we'd jam and record. I remember talking about taking it on the road but nothing ever came of it. It was too bad. There was some really good material there, but it wasn't recorded well and the mixes were terrible. Nick would have benefited from having a singer other than himself, but he really wanted to do it all himself. Those were pretty dark days for him and for me too.

My dad helped me out on the record, mixing and listening to the recordings. I needed that since I was so close to it and doubted everything. I couldn't settle on any mixes, and I had to have somebody else there, saying, "Yeah, that's good." Max was amazing and offered me a lot of advice and encouragement, but he couldn't be there full time. Dad kept telling me, "Be done with it."

I thought I was going to master it myself, but no way. In the end, I wasn't happy with any of the mixes and was never happy with my voice. There are things that I wish I could change, but it is what it is. It's just a snapshot in time. My singing's *ok.* I think that's the least talented thing on my record—the vocals—but I was able to settle with them and let it go. The next one will be better; that's all I can say.

I didn't even look for a label. I was so fed up with Megadeth's record label at the time and how much money was being thrown away and the lack of camaraderie between record company and band. Nobody really cares. Capitol Records was poorly pushing us, as far as tour support and all that stuff, and we were un-recouped. The money that goes through your hands to the record people, it's like, "Where did it go? Can somebody please tell me where it goes?"

It's like 60 percent of our records were gone right off the top. You think, "Man, we got a shitty deal."

I was looking at Prince and all these people going internal and on the internet selling records themselves. I thought, "You know what? I have life after Deth. There's life for me because I can go do whatever I want to do."

So, I started working on my record, thinking, "If I sell ten percent of what I could sell in Megadeth, that's like 100,000 records. If I sell that much, which I know I have at least ten percent of the fans out there who will buy my record, that would be fine. I could do a record a year, tour, and that would be all I'd need."

I boycotted record companies. I signed myself to my own record company. I am the record company, the A&R person, the producer, and all that. What's more is that I can't be dropped!

It seemed like a plan to me. Gallo, Ty, and Jason and I had fully planned on taking it out and playing some gigs, doing a tour of at least California, but the absolute unthinkable happened. Ty took a few months off from our rehearsals to go on the road with the re-forming Great White and was one of one hundred people killed in that nightclub fire in Rhode Island. That was horrifying. It knocked the wind out of everybody's sails. Ty was a great guy who had a young son. That was one of the biggest tragedies ever—all those people dying for such a stupid reason.

The next year, Jason died of heart failure. I don't understand anybody that young dying of heart failure, but when he died after Ty's tragedy, I was done. I shelved all plans. It was too painful to go back and revisit that stuff. I've been asked by labels in the years since to remaster it and repackage it and put it out, but it's done. It was a lot of fun to record, and I was looking forward to the live shows. I even thought about fronting the band at one point and bringing somebody else to play drums, but I had to move past it. It's history.

I wasn't aspiring with that record to have any Top-10 singles or anything like that. The record was just something I needed to get out of my system and out of my head. It was an exorcism; total autobiographical therapy for my own sake. If you look at all the song titles, you can see it pertains to those past ten years. There are a couple songs about the people in my life at that time, but it's mostly about my life and my experiences. I'd just wanted to go out and tour and survive on it. But the cold reality of just how difficult it is to market your own record by yourself sank in. You really can't do it all alone. I shouldn't have been so surprised, but I was in the Megadeth bubble for so long I began to believe it was all as easy as it looked. It ain't. I don't want to be an executive; I just want to make music and play it for people.

During this time in my personal life, my girlfriend Terri and I welcomed sons Nicholas and, a few years later, Donte, into the world. With them, everything changed. Music, my career, everything took on a whole new perspective, and the only thing that ever has really mattered to me since has been the boys. They are my focus—everything else comes after, which is the way it's supposed to be. Family first.

If only I hadn't been so brutally thrown off course. Shortly before Donte was born, somebody came over to the house and offered me a drag on a meth pipe. I'd never really fucked with hard drugs or been interested in them—not after seeing the colossal damage they'd done to Mustaine. But I like to smoke pot, and I thought, "What the fuck? Let's see what this is all about."

One deep inhale, and everything changed. Forever.

I was trapped. I was a hostage in that dark tunnel blocked off from emotions, reason, and reality for a few years, getting worse every month until my family finally stepped in. Terri tried, of course, but for a brief time, she too started having substance issues amidst having to compensate for my absence with caring for Nicholas. I thank God, Buddha, the Great Drummer in the Sky—whatever you call her—that nothing terrible happened, and Nicholas was never neglected or put in harm's way.

With Donte, Nicholas, and Terri at my Mom and Dad's place in Studio City.

By the time Donte was born, I was very ill. I was emotionally crippled and vacant. Nothing in life ever seemed so exciting and plugged-in and vibrant than when I smoked meth. Nothing replaces it when you're in its grasp. We're not meant to feel that good, to have our brains so short-circuited. It was the darkest struggle of my life. Getting fired from Megadeth was nothing compared to what the drugs did to me, but the compounding trouble and the whole trap was that I was in such a low place that the drugs seemed like the only positive and exciting thing I could do. The meth replaced the high of being a father or of being on stage performing for people. It's the worst lie I have ever experienced. It cost me my family. Terri finally couldn't take it anymore, and she couldn't get clean with me using, so she took our boys and moved out. It was nothing like you'd imagine. There was no big fight or drama. I didn't want it to happen and tried to work through it with her, but it just wasn't in the cards when I was so sick. We were friends then, and we're friends to this day; and I go and see Nicholas and Donte often where they live in the Pacific Northwest. I stay at the house and cook breakfasts, and we do Menza Taco Nights and have a blast. Everyone's healthy and happy and mighty, and it's beautiful. I'm so enormously grateful, because it could have turned out so tragically.

I stumbled through a long series of sessions and one-off appearances on records by the Greek Megadeth wannabe band Memorain and then the Pantera-sound-alike band Orphaned To Hatred, for which I played on the album *War Plow*. At the time, I did it because there was nothing else going on, and because I was so depressed and desperate I thought trading on my legacy was a good idea. In the end, it was all just easy for me to do, and the only thing it did was embarrass me because people didn't take them for what they should have been. I'm not saying anything bad about anybody, because there's nothing bad to say.

All the guys are friends and have been forever. They're awesome, and they're great players and they had their hearts in the right place, but looking back, I don't think it's where we should have been putting our talents. We should have been doing something new, something far more original. Orphaned To Hatred was meant as Bob Zilla's tribute to his bandmate Dimebag Darrell, and there's nothing wrong with that. But a lot of fans just thought we were trading on Pantera's legacy, not performing a tribute. It doesn't matter what the truth is. The fans are always right, dude.

I take responsibility for my part in why those projects failed. I wasn't in a state of mind to be making good decisions. I don't regret making those albums; I just wish we'd done something else. I'm sure the fans do, too. Through all these dark days, there were a few bands I thought about joining, if they'd have me. One was Linkin Park. I loved the band back in the day and would have joined them in a heartbeat, but the only time there was a vacancy was when Dave Farrell briefly left the band.

There was a shot I took at joining Opeth—them or Porcupine were two metal bands I would have joined because they would have been a natural evolution of everything I'd done in Megadeth rather than just joining a band doing the same kind of thing or mimicking somebody else. In late 2005, Martin Lopez walked away from Opeth, and I immediately threw my hat into the ring.

I was without management at the time, so I contacted their office in Sweden myself. It's the only time I ever used the Megadeth name to try to score a gig, despite everyone encouraging me to use it all the time.

It backfired. Right away I got grief from their road manager, who emailed me saying, "It's really not cool to say you're Nick Menza when you're not!"

I wrote right back and said, "What the fuck are you talking about? I *am* Nick Menza!"

Then Peter Lindgren emailed me and said something like, "Dude, is this really you?"

I wrote, "I'll come and play with you right now!"

It was totally like, "Will the real Nick Menza please sit down!"

Fuck. It didn't happen, obviously. That would have been cool. Still, it would have been back to the metal drumming (which I love, don't get me wrong), but I did that my whole career before I was forced to take a long break and be a real human being. For a long time now it's been weighing on me to get out there and stretch myself, do something challenging that

I've never done before. See if I can really do it and prove myself outside of metal.

I guess the first real move in that direction happened when I teamed up with some old friends again in a band called Deltanaut. It was a band of dudes I went to high school with: Brian Hacksaw Williams on vocals, my old pal Chris Grady on guitar, Colin Reid on guitar, and Darwin Ballard (who'd been in the very first bands I was in) played bass. That was a project that really took me in a new direction. We did a full record out at Sound City, which was awesome, but we had the resources to mix and master only about five of the tunes. We did one video for a tune called *Sacrifice*, which is clearly a huge departure for me. It was cool. My dad came in and played the sax solo on a tune called "The King."

Deltanaut

Chris has always been one of my best buds and is a great guitar player. He wrote most of the material, which we described as "Heavy Mellow." That worked out well because it was the first band I was in after I cut my arm badly in an accident. It was perfect, really, since I couldn't play all that hard for any prolonged period. My arm was still fucked up, but the doctors had told me I'd never play again, so I wasn't complaining.

We did gigs around L.A. and got some attention. We even got an offer to go to the Middle East and play the Persian Gulf on Christmas morning for some USO shows. I was stoked, but the other dudes were not into it. I'd do it. I may still go sometime if I ever have another offer to. I'd play for the troops anywhere, anytime.

The thing about Deltanaut was that as cool as the other dudes were and the fact that I was into a departure musically, my head wasn't together and I was heading into the worst part of my drug darkness.

Around the same time, I played on a tune that Anthony Gallo wrote for Mindstreem called "We Up Next," which was an interesting move into a more hip-hop/metal blend. I thought it was cool, and I would be into doing more stuff like that. The way I play, I bring heavy to whatever I touch, no matter what style of music it is. That's what I like to be known most for—my style of playing and my abilities, not necessarily who I've played with in the past or who I'm playing with in the moment.

As time progressed, I was having trouble finding my place again in music. I produced a lot of dudes, did guest spots, drum clinics, gave lessons, and it seems every year there's an offer to do tribute tours with other legacy metal players. It always seems like a good idea at the time and then collapses under the weight of crooked promoters. It's sad and depressing. If it doesn't feel right, however, I won't do it. It's not worth it to my peace of mind. I have lived and learned enough to discover that I just need balance: the balance of my boys, my family, my friends, and my health. And my art.

WHAT'S IN A NAME?

Am I proud of my decade with Megadeth? You bet. That lineup of Dave Mustaine, Dave Ellefson, Marty Friedman, and me *is* Megadeth, the band that most of the fans still clamor for. We had it all: platinum albums and incredible world tours supporting or being supported by some of the best acts in rock. It was a dream come true.

But do I like it when one of my sons proudly boasts that his Dad is "Nick Menza from Megadeth?" Not really. *Cringe.* I don't like anyone thinking of me in as one-dimensional. I've been out of Megadeth for more years than I was with the band, and as amazing a time as it was, I can't let it define me.

As a musician, I'm far more than a former drummer for Megadeth. I play R&B, jazz, pop, and hard rock. Shit, I'll play country if I think the session is hot.

I have to tell you, it ain't easy seeing the way people sometimes react when they hear the word Megadeth. It's not exactly a PG-13, grandma-friendly name. Metallica is a cooler name.

You want to be massive. You want to be a household name, but for some people, when they hear Megadeth, it's like, "How nice for you. You worship the devil, right?"

I remember being on a flight out of L.A., enjoying relative peace and quiet in between the occasional kid coming up from coach and asking for my autograph. It's always cool when you get to talk to a fan. I was sitting next to this interesting looking woman who I couldn't take my eyes off of, when I embarrassingly realized it was Björk.

She asked me what band I was with (between the autographs and the hair, it was obvious something was up).

"Megadeth," I said.

"Oh." Her face dropped. "I don't like that kind of music."

I was used to hearing this response from "civilians," as I liked to call them. I wasn't offended.

"Nah, me neither," I said with a smile.

She looked at me kind of strangely. I reached into the bag I had under the seat, got my sleeve of CDs, pulled out her *Post* record, and asked if she'd sign it for me.

Björk turned beet red and stammered something of an excuse about what she'd said, that she hoped she didn't offend me. She was blown away that I had her CD with me and that the "drummer from Megadeth" was into her music. Well, I liked that second record a lot and just so happened to be listening to it around that time. She was cool, but weird looking, man! I kept gazing at her throughout the flight. Sometimes she looked really cute. She'd get up, go to the lavatory, come back and, something about the light and I'd think, "Ah, nope." It was trippy. She kept changing. Like a chameleon. I later saw a Seinfeld episode in which Jerry's girlfriend was just like that!

Once, on a flight to London, I sat next to this sweet, elderly American lady. We were enjoying some small talk, and she said her name was Beatrice. She was lovely. She mentioned her son was in music. I said, "Oh, really, what does he do? Would I know him?"

She beamed and said, "You might. He plays guitar. His name is Bob Dylan."

I was like, "No way! Your son is Bob Dylan! You're joking! That's so cool!"

We talked for some time, and she told me proudly about how he'd bought a nice house for her in Arizona, where she spent winters. Finally, she asked, "What's the name of your band?"

"Megadeth," I said before even giving pause to what her reaction might be. She didn't say another word, but she turned her head and didn't speak to me for the duration of the flight.

I tried for a few minutes to make small talk, ask for a cup of tea for her, but I didn't exist anymore. I became Megadeth Man and, in her mind, probably barbecued babies on the weekends or some other heinous devil-worshipping behavior. So sad. I hate when that happens.

Years later, after I was out of Megadeth and had largely left the metal world behind, I was tipped off that John Mayer was looking for a new drummer. I was so wary of the "Nick Menza from Megadeth" label that I just went in and talked to John's management and tried to sell them on *Nick* and hope they gave me even a minute on a drum kit. I knew they would have said, "No, we're not interested," at the first syllable of "Megadeth." My efforts fell brutally short, however. The next day I got a call and this dude said, "You didn't think we'd find out who you are?"

"Well," I answered, "what does *that* have anything to do with John Mayer? I can do the gig, man. I can play anything you throw at me."

"Sorry."

"You mean you're not going to give me an audition because of what band I used to play with?"

"Yeah, pretty much. You're not what we're looking for."

I didn't say it, but inside I was bursting to respond, "Oh, really? I thought you'd be looking for someone who's talented and could play the music. After playing in Megadeth, I can play any kind of music. Any style!" It wouldn't have changed a thing. The stereotyping sucks. And it sucked even more so when it was a gig I really thought I had a shot at because of Megadeth. Ozzy was looking for a new band, and my name came up with Sharon, who is absolutely incredible and who has always been great to me. Ozzy's always been the same, too, really cool to me. The Godfather!

Unfortunately, Dave had recently said something in the press slamming Ozzy's use of teleprompters on stage, and Ozzy was pissed at any whiff of Mustaine or Megadeth. "Nick Menza" was an awesome name to Sharon and to Ozzy both, right up until Sharon answered his question, "Who's he played with?" Ozzy reportedly yelled that no one was to mention Nick Menza again. Not fair to me, but I understand. It was to be a huge challenge to stretch out beyond Megadeth no matter what I did. And nearly impossible, sometimes, if I was auditioning for anyone who had ever met or knew Mustaine personally.

CHAPTER SEVEN

"I PLEDGE ALLEGIANCE..."

"I pledge allegiance to the frequencies of the United Field of Acoustics and to the vibrations for which they sound on sine wave, under oscillation, invisible with equal and just tuning for all."

It's all about the sounds, the rhythms, the feeling, the art; the creation. Nothing that's made strictly for the money has any magic to it. Money's nice, but I'd rather do something I love and be so good at it that people will pay me to keep doing it.

I've had a life of drumming and music. Aside from a dark time when I didn't want to play, listen to, or think about music—or anything, for that matter—music has been my greatest passion.

Well, aside from my two sons. I love doing projects with them. We once did a science experiment together where we took some leftover sushi and put half in a container with a label that read "Love" and the other in a container labeled "Hate." After about a month, the LOVE sushi was covered in this fluffy white mold, and the HATE sushi was infested with this heinous black shit. That was cool.

Lurking below the surface in me is an unending desire to do stuff, build stuff, create stuff, invent stuff; paint stuff. I can't sit still. It's hard for me to even make it all the way through a movie before I'm bored and start thinking of ways to make movies, or how to make the theater seats more comfortable or some shit like that.

I get my frustrations out by playing drums; it helps me to relax and clear my mind. Art of any kind does the same thing for me. I love it. There are some apps on my phone that I can make art with, which is really cool when I'm in airplanes or at the airport or whatever. That's a way to seriously burn up some time being creative when you're jammed up somewhere you don't want to be and can't do anything else.

At home, every week I do something to feed the insatiable monster of creation by coming up with something I've never done or thought of before. So after a show or a rehearsal or if I'm burned out from practicing, I find myself getting into all kinds of creative nonsense.

Christian Nesmith:
Nick's mind never stopped. He was always brainstorming. "What about this?" At the time music videos were starting to break out and Tommy Lee was doing his upside-down drum solos, Nick wanted to top Tommy. He had this idea about having this military plane (the kind that has the back that opens up in flight) having his whole kit bolted down to a riser, coming out the back of the plane with parachutes on each end to keep it steady, and he'd parachute down to the platform, play a solo, and then dive off. He'd have cameras properly placed on the ground to film the drum set being demolished. I mean, how rock 'n' roll is that? Nick was never short of ideas. He wanted to do glass cymbals in a video, so that he'd come around on a drum fill and super slow motion and he'd hit the cymbal and it would shatter. He had ideas like that all the time.

I go through phases, I guess, like painting. I've painted for most of my life, everything from oils and acrylics to watercolors and mixed media pieces where I glue found objects onto my canvases. I've done sculptures in metal, and once I get going on papier-mâché, it's hard to stop me. I wish it were Halloween every weekend, because I carve the most gnarly and frightening pumpkins imaginable. I love that shit.

My first public display, I guess you'd say, was when I was asked to participate in the 1994 *Musicians As Artists* book, which was an awesome honor. I'm as proud of being in that book as I am anything else I've done. It's me along with Tony Bennett, Jerry Garcia, Miles Davis, Ringo Starr, Roger Waters, Iggy Pop, Ron Wood, John Lennon, John Mellencamp, David Bowie, Jon Anderson, and Donna Summer.

I studied sculpture, graphic arts, oils, and acrylics and found that painting was a release for any of the inner frustration that I couldn't get out on drums.

I just paint whatever. I never say, "Okay, I'm going to paint a dog now." I just start working and see what comes out. It's very ad lib, free form, abstract. I don't even have a favorite artist. It's sort of like music in that way, and my attention span is just as brief. I find it hard to be really satisfied with anything I do and probably paint ten different paintings on the same canvas before I finally come up with the one I like. My family and friends come by and say, "Where's that painting you had yesterday?" I tell them I've painted over it, and they get all annoyed.

"But I liked that one," they say. But I didn't. I'm the artist, and I have to like it. My music's the same. I do take after take and mess with tempos and rhythms because usually only one is just right.

I think in the next twenty years, the only sane people on the planet are going to be the artists. Everyone else is too caught up in the system. Survival will mean living and being outside the system.

The biggest thing I've done in a few years now is a collaborative project with a company here in L.A. called SceneFour. I'm one of the latest drummers they've brought on board to do a series of mixed analog-digital mixed media that captures our rhythms on canvas or whatever.

They put me in a room with these lighted drumsticks and asked me to play while they did a long-exposure photo of me, about 30 seconds, drumming in a totally blacked-out room. Later we checked out the images, and I picked the ones that represent me or tell an interesting story. They did their magic on the computer, adjusting all the layers and colors and histograms to bring out the image that I saw there with my eyes. It goes to print or canvas from there.

One of my unsold masterpieces on the wall of Megadeth's studio in Phoenix, Arizona.

You know humans are preprogrammed—we see images, especially faces or creatures, in just about anything—clouds, ocean waves, cereal, carpet, or whatever. I think we're all inhabited by other entities, and they come through and inform our behavior and our choices. Places aren't haunted—people are haunted. We see shit whether it's there or not. For instance, there's one rhythm canvas I did called *Area 51* that has these alien skulls reaching out from the picture. There's another called *Dragon* that I did with Mylar drumheads I made. I used red and orange LED-triggered drumsticks. I used Mylar on another one, with the LED sticks and fiber-optic brushes. It's awesome.

Steven Adler, Mickey Hart, Bill Ward, Chad Smith, Matt Sorum, Dave Lombardo, Carl Palmer, Carmine Appice, Chad Sexton, Jose Pasillas, Mike Mangini, Billy Cobham and I are the latest to do them. Mine goes up for sale this summer, on my birthday, July 23, and the whole collection I think is going to be in a show that goes all over the country. These guys Cory Danziger and Ravi Dosaj are behind it all. It's very cool; check it out.

Woodworking is another thing that's been a passion of mine for most of my adult life. From building furniture to home renovations—I'm redoing all my kitchen cabinets right now—and art pieces, it's something I seriously enjoy. I've designed the last few drum kits that DC California Drums has made for me. Actually, it was Soultone Cymbals and DC drums owner Iki Levy who came up to me one day and said, "Can you make a box?"

I was like, "Outta what?"

He went and brought out a cajón and showed it to me. I'd seen them played by Latin jazz dudes. They're Peruvian. I looked at it and said, "Yeah, it's a three-ply birch on the sides you play on, and the rest is half-inch whatever, maple; mahogany. I can make one, sure."

The first few I made didn't sound all that good because I wasn't aware of the wood grain flowing together. When you cut a board into separate pieces they have to be aligned when you put them together or the resonance isn't going along the wood grain. Putting random pieces together is the first mistake. I discovered that I had to think of it as if I could just roll one long piece of wood up into a box. That's the secret.

I make all kinds of different shapes and sizes. A lot of them I sell to a drum store here in the Valley and started selling like five or six at a time. It has started to really take off and now I'm doing ten at a time and pumping them out so fast I don't even take pictures of most of them. It

was just a cool thing to do, you know, but now my friend Allen, who has been helping me with some of the structural designs and technical stuff over at his shop, is working with me on a plan to actually go into full cajón production for real—the Nick Menza Cajóns.

It's rad. Every one is unique, with different ornamentation—even electronics if people want. I now have so many different styles and designs. The bass ones are huge.

I'm planning on making a table set, like a dinner set. Imagine having a bunch of drummers sitting around playing this little drum symphony of cajóns. How cool would that be, right?

Designing my own drums was a natural segue into designing my own cymbal line. I'd always wanted to have a signature line with Soultone, because I am absolutely a cymbal snob. Cymbals have to be like a really good meal. Here's what I mean: There's got to be a great beginning when you first hit the cymbal, a great follow through with the splash or crash or ring of the ride, and it's got to end perfectly, with an abrupt fade, a slow wash or lasting ring or whatever. Just as every cymbal has its purpose, it's got to fulfill every one of the requirements of that purpose perfectly for me. Machine-made cymbals just don't meet every one of those requirements.

Iki's family's Soultone cymbals do, which is why I use them and endorse them. He's taught me just about everything I know about cymbals and has given me rejects to experiment on for my personal line. I use grinders, files, and saws and have been experimenting with high-pressure water-jet engraving, salt-water engraving, and laser engraving. It's amazing. Not too surprising, it's easy to fuck up a cymbal.

After practicing on dozens of spoils from the shop, I've been able to get enough experience that I can now get the sounds I'm after with the designs I'm after. One complements the other. No two cymbals are alike, of course, since they're all handmade, and my designs are either done by hand or in a combination of machine engraver and hand painting.

It all started with this show on television about these vibrational frequency patterns on these scopes. Every time the sound came up it would make all these different designs, and I thought, "That's what I need to do on my cymbals."

I'm totally into the pyramid thing. I just didn't know how to go about achieving what I was seeing in my head. I tried all kinds of things. Finally, a disc sander was the thing. It lets me get the lines I want, rounded and three-dimensional. Like life, and all things, you just can't be afraid to try. I couldn't be afraid to grind down a few cymbals and wreck them. You have to be fearless to adventure into new things. That's how discoveries are made, even if it's just to make a cymbal look rad. When I started, I really didn't have a clue about what I wanted them to look like, so I worked with some cymbals of mine that had cracks in them or that I didn't like. I nailed it after a few prototypes, learning which tools to use and how to get the hologram kind of look when they move as you hit them. They bounce back and look sick.

Iki was mad at me at first. "What have you done! They're all fucked up!"

"They're *my* cymbals, dude, relax. They sound great."

Then he heard them. "Those sound *amazing!*"

Now doing the Nick Menza Signature line.

I get bored easily and have refinished most of my guitars too. Boredom is absolutely the mother of creation when it comes to me, especially on the road. On off days, like a Sunday when all the shops are closed in so many countries, I'd take down the paintings in my room, take them out of their frames, draw in little spaceships, and stick them back up on the wall. I must have done hundreds of them. They'd have lame artwork like a beach and a wave. I'd get out my metallic pens and draw in little spaceships with lights on them. That's a great way to pass the time, wondering who—days, weeks, or months later—would notice. I should have taken pictures of them. A few were awesome—a city scene with a spaceship up in the corner, just big enough people would look at them and go, "Hey, Mildred, hand me my glasses. Look at this. Am I seeing things?"

After the first couple of tours, the excitement was pretty much gone unless I was on stage. (Well, unless I was on stage or Marty and I had hit

Pottery for Pets...making cool junk for charity.

one of our favorite Korean or sushi places in whatever town we were in.) I had to keep myself busy.

I still do it when I'm on the road for any time, no matter where I am and no matter what I'm doing. Here's an example, something I've never told many people. If you're out fishing somewhere in Southern California and catch a fish with a little silver "M" tagged on one of its fins, that's me doing a little artistic high-five to nature and the world.

I started tagging the fish I catch (I always catch and release) with these cool little silver "M" buttons I designed. That's "M" for *Menza*, dude. I don't fish as much as I once did, but still, my "fish" art is out there. If you ever catch one, keep the narrative going. Take a selfie with the fish, and release it back into the wild. That's you and me collaborating on some art of nature.

I do all these art experiments to keep from going mad. Life itself is art (or at least it should be), and art itself has to have life of its own. If it's good it'll touch at least one other person. Art is the only way to immortality, though you can't do it for that reason. Immortality is something that just happens as a result of art.

Juan Alvarez:
Nick was a driver, a motivator. He was the instigator. He never let up. Through his entire life he was like that. I would still go over to his house near the end, and he'd be inventing things, building things, making new sounds and new ways of doing things. He'd make snares out of different things, like brass. And he'd paint all his drums and refinish them in different ways, making them sound different. The guy was relentless.

WOULDN'T YOU?

Some things are hard to resist. The smell of bacon slays me. (My favorite guitar quote is from Bonnie Raitt, who once said her vintage Strat "sounds like bacon smells!")

I have never found anything more irresistible than legendary drum kits. When Megadeth was at Masterfonics Studio in Nashville in 1996–1997 rehearsing, writing, and doing some recording for what was first called *Pins and Needles* but ended up being the *Cryptic Writings* record, one of the engineers said he needed to make a run down to Studio Instruent Rentals to get some more microphones. He let drop that they owned one of John Bonham's kits.

I was *so* there!

It was one of those amber translucent Ludwig Vistalite kits that look great and sound like shit. It was set up in one of the hallways, and there was no one who was going to keep me from jumping on it. It was righteous! I started thundering away, doing one of those classic Bonham stuttered pedal things on the bass. One of the guys from SIR said, "Oh, man, everyone plays the same fucking beat!"

Oh yeah! "When the Levee Breaks." "The Rover." It was so cool.

I went a few steps further when we were in Tel Aviv once. I went out on one of our "non-performance" nights to the Hard Rock. I was sitting there having a drink and chatting up some of the locals and tourists when I noticed this drum kit set up on a balcony above the bar. It was a sort of creamy white Premiere set with gold fittings.

"Is that Keith Moon's kit?" I asked somebody behind the bar.

"Yeah, it is. That's the one he gave to Ringo Starr."

I was down! Well, up, actually. I climbed up on the bar and up onto the balcony and started bashing away. The kit was awesome, though it wasn't in very good shape and the heads and cymbals sucked. The patrons seemed to love it, but the staff of the Hard Rock didn't. They were all motioning and yelling at me to come down for fear the balcony would collapse. *Whatever!* I thought.

It's amazing how differently you can set up a drum kit. I've found that it varies greatly from drummer to drummer. Some dudes set their stuff up in ways that other people find it really difficult to play—like my ultimate hero Buddy Rich. When I was a teenager, I set Buddy's kit up a few times—once at the Hollywood Bowl for the Playboy Jazz Festival. I sure couldn't play it, though. I don't know how Buddy did it (I don't know how Buddy did just about anything on the drum kit) but with his setup, I was pretty much hopeless at making my way around or getting a sound or any power. Everything about him was humbling.

Don Menza:

I was doing *Cats* down in the Schubert Theater, and I took two weeks off to do a tour with Buddy. I showed up with Nick, and he said, "This is Nick?" Nick was fifteen years old by then, and the last time Buddy had seen him he was probably four or five. We'd gone up to play San Francisco and then on our way back south to do the Playboy Festival at the Hollywood Bowl. I said, "Buddy, I need some passes for my son." Buddy said, "Well, I'll tell you what, he and a couple of other guys carry all the drums and set them up—he knows where I want them and everything—and it's a deal." So, Nick had all-access passes. People were waiting for Buddy Rich, and Nick is up there getting the drums set up. It was funny.

CHAPTER EIGHT

BUT ARE THEY ILLEGAL ALIENS?

I've never been probed, but I did go out with a couple of chicks that were aliens.

I'll always be known as the "drummer from Megadeth" no matter how many years I've been out of the band. I embrace that now and am particularly proud for being recognized for "Hangar 18." I wrote the lyrics that inspired Dave to recycle a "Call of Ktulu" riff from his Metallica days into a new song for *Rust In Peace*, and it's now one of the most lasting hits we ever had.

In the video, the aliens get tortured and we all end up frozen. I got the idea from the movie *Hangar 18*, about a crashed UFO that the government hides from the public. A real stretch, right?

Since I was a kid, I was into outer space and the stars and have always believed that a UFO crashed at Roswell in the late 1940s. I believe that two dead alien bodies and one live one were taken to Hangar 18 at Wright-Patterson Air Force Base in Ohio. They were later moved to Area 51 for research and are still there.

Extra-terrestrials, UFOs, and conspiracies became general topics of tolerance by Junior and Marty, but like just about everything, they became a source of annoyance for Dave. None of it was Dave's favorite topic of conversation, and he's a really easy dude to annoy. I love getting a rise out of people, to see whether or not they take me seriously no matter what I say, or dismiss everything I say just because I do believe some *crazy* things.

Marty Friedman:
Nick and his aliens. Although I always thought he was way too intelligent for all that stuff, there was something kind of lovable about how he stuck to these nutty conspiracy stories. I believe it gave him an identity that stood out, so he played that stuff up. Thankfully none of the rest of us held it against him, and it was always a source of fun for everyone. Nick definitely inspired the song, "Hangar 18" which was one of our most popular tunes. Nick was the alien guy, I was the Japan nerd; David was the Vulgarian because he swore so much. I'm not really sure what Dave was.

After going through his whole devil-worship phase, Dave became a Christian, probably because he saw that it was one of the things that turned Junior's life around. Whether it's done him any good is anyone's guess by looking at his behavior—or his tweets. I could so easily get under his skin, though, by telling him that Jesus or his mother Mary could have been aliens, as I said earlier. I *do* believe in a historical figure named Jesus. For sure he walked this earth and at least tried to tell us all how to act right, not that most people these days are paying attention to the fine print.

It pissed Dave off, though. He didn't like me talking about it, especially in the press.

No one outside of the system has proof, or this wouldn't be the huge conspiracy it is. I believe it's a conspiracy because we as a society aren't prepared for any of the real truths about what our governments know, what they do, and what they have planned for us.

I *love* conspiracies. There have been UFO sightings since Biblical times, and nothing in this life is simply as it appears, dude. Rattle 'em

off: Planet X, Aliens (The Anunnaki, The Nordics Greys, Reptilians), the JFK assassination, the 9/11 cover-up, cloud seeding, viruses, faked moon landings, the Illuminati, and, of course, one of the biggest, the "round Earth" conspiracy orchestrated by the government and NASA. Count me in. I like just about any conspiracy theory, unless it comes with a website with merchandise.

The last poll I saw said 70 percent of Americans don't believe Lee Harvey Oswald acted alone. And if you believe one conspiracy, that opens your mind to the possibilities of others. The American government has admitted MK-Ultra, the program where the CIA did a bunch of secret tests on people with LSD and then tried to cover it up by destroying all the files in the early 1970s in the panic over the whole Nixon Watergate scandal. That's not a theory; it's a well-documented incident.

People are always coming up to me asking me about aliens, whether I've heard about this sighting or that sighting. I get asked a lot about conspiracies and what I think's really going on with the government. I tell them, "What if I talk about what I know and they hear? They'll come to my house and shut me down and it will be like, 'Whatever happened to that dude?'" I have seen things in the sky nearly every time I've driven to and from Vegas. Out there in the middle of the desert at night, there are things to be seen that defy explanation.

Recently, I was driving back to L.A. at about 3:30 in the morning, and off in the distance there was what looked like a windstorm. I pulled over and got out of the car to get a better look. It was eerie. There was a small point of light and a glow around it. It moved up and down the mountain range so quickly I could barely keep track of it. Finally, I thought that it was probably not a good idea to just stand there alone.

It was not a good experience. Spooky is not always good, dude.

A lot of people think my house is haunted. I've never seen anything, at least when I've been in a clear state of mind. But so many people tell me the place has a lot of conflicting energy. Dogs and cats *hate* my kitchen for some reason. They'll run through it on the way to the studio if they're following me, or run through it on the way out of the studio, but they won't hang out there—even if there's food around.

I've seen all kinds of shit that I can't explain. Do I know what I saw? No. But I can't explain it, and it's not stuff you see every day. Most of it defies description except to say that it is not from this world. It hasn't been something I've enjoyed.

There's a really cool L.A. singer-songwriter named Michele Vreeland. We were talking about doing some sessions. She came over to the house one day, and right away she said, "Dude, there's something definitely going on in here. It's an item that you've got in the house. You need to get rid of some of the skulls and things. I don't see many pictures of your kids. Maybe you should have more family stuff."

I took Michele's advice. I've always believed that things have spirits, or memories, attached to them, even if I've never knowingly experienced it. Supernatural occurrences and conspiracies are in our intelligent nature: where there's a vacuum for an explanation, we'll grab onto anything that fits the hole, no matter how improbable it might seem.

If you take a step back with an open mind and think about history, aliens make sense. They're our modern version of fairies. That may sound nuts since we're living in the Disney-fied version of life, but if you read some of the old fairy tales, some of the elves weren't cute little people. They were the ones who put Rip Van Winkle to sleep. Not all the fairies of old are sweet little pixies that flutter around our heads with dreamy blessings. Sometimes they eat us.

That's the modern fairy tale—alien abduction. Creatures that are beyond our understanding and intelligence and who have powers and abilities we can't fathom. We're their playthings, if you think the worst. To me, space aliens are far scarier than the devil. I'm far more worried aliens are going to come down here and eat us or put us in a zoo. What scares me is being cattle for the aliens.

My friend Allen Hall and I did a fake UFO sighting video with my sons for the fun of it a couple of years ago and posted it on YouTube. It was a harmless prank, but when I started getting interview requests from TV stations and newspapers all over the world, we got nervous and took it down. We were going to do a whole series of them, but it got carried away really quickly. Maybe it wasn't such a good idea, because it helped cast doubt on all the legitimate sighting videos. But I like getting people to question things and talk about all the possibilities of what might be out there.

Allen Hall:
Nick liked to spin people up over conspiracy theories and aliens on purpose, just so he could get a rise out of me arguing that it was nonsense. We were planning a follow-up video of him being abducted. I wish we had found the time to do that. It would have been hilarious.

One of the coolest projects I've ever been involved with was courtesy of my old bandmate John "Gumby" Goodwin, who wrote a major documentary called *UFOs Above and Beyond* and brought me in to produce it with him for the Learning Channel. The show has more than one hundred and fifty photos and one hundred videos, some of which had never been seen before. We managed to get Scotty from *Star Trek* (actor James Doohan) to host and narrate, which was pretty great except that during the production it was hard to keep him sober. We couldn't get through too many takes before he'd start slurring his words.

The show was a success. I wish it had turned into a whole series, because there's enough stuff out there to investigate.

I really don't think we've set foot on the moon. What's more likely: that men flew to the moon almost half a century ago and made it back here? or it was all faked on a soundstage by Stanley Kubrick?

We're not supposed to leave the earth. We're not space-bound bodies. As soon as we leave the earth's atmosphere, we'd be microwaved instantly. A few years ago, the Chinese landed a probe on the moon right where one of the Apollo landings was supposed to be, and they didn't find any evidence of anything having been there. Just look at the photographs it sent back, the panoramic shots. It's so lame. Nice rendering in the background. You can see where they cut the mountains in the background. Nice try. We've never been to the moon. We'll never leave this planet. We'll never be able to make it to Mars. You'd need like a six-foot lead capsule to keep from being fried by the Van Allen Radiation Belt, and it would be so heavy we'd never get it off the ground. Dude, we're held together by gravity. Up there, our bodies would fail. Our organs would fail.

I think we are evolving as a race with our technological advancements, ascending to a new level of consciousness, but there's a lot of stuff we have no business messing with—like nuclear technology. We do *not* have that shit dialed in, and I don't think we ever will. We're not God, and we shouldn't pretend to be by screwing with atoms like that. We've got solar, wind, and ocean currents for generating electricity. We shouldn't be burning coal or oil or messing with nukes. Nothing good will ever come of that. Look at Fukashima. I read one study that said basically every living thing on the planet has received two x-rays worth of radiation from that nuke meltdown. Dude, you think I eat anything coming out of the Pacific Ocean? Ever? Think again.

With the Illuminati and world-order groups like Bilderberg, I don't doubt there are master plans for total authoritarian control. With ever-increasing phone updates and chips being implanted in everything it will soon be everyone. Forget vaccines—we're going to get chipped, and there's nothing we can do about it, whether you understand the math or not.

I'm down for the ride!

Is Stevie Wonder really totally blind? Just look at some of the videos of him on YouTube. It's all about imagination and possibilities. And I'm an optimist in this life. A conspiracy theory does not have to be untrue. In my world, possibility equals probability. From Easter Island to Stonehenge or the Pyramids, there's a lot that's real and unexplained around us.

The U.S. Government's HAARP (High Frequency Active Auroral Research Program) started in the early 1990s, and a decade later it was capable of creating artificial northern lights in the sky. You think that's a good thing? At the very best-case scenario, they're using it to catalogue every living being on the planet so they can know who drinks Pepsi and who drinks Coke. Wait until there's advertising all across our skies at night. They have already used barium holograms in the sky, which are pretty freaky when they're religious images being projected. Imagine the hysteria that could cause (of course, at its worst, electromagnetic weapons). Which one do you think the military's most interested in? They say the huge antennae array in Alaska was shut down a couple of years ago, but no one says the whole program has stopped. Anything that falls under what the feds call "national security" is bound to be bad for somebody.

Is there anything we can do about it? No, dude. You can wrap foil around your head if you like, but I'm not going to. It wouldn't work anyway.

Now, just because things are invisible doesn't mean they're evil or bad. Sound waves can be used for either healing or hurting. They call it vibrational healing, and it's been around for thousands of years. That's what the government should really be looking into developing. Wouldn't

it be an ideal world if all we had to do to overcome illness and disease was to lie back and listen to beautiful music?

> **Robert Bolger, (Nick's manager):**
> God, I miss Nick's endless pranks and jokes. I could go on for days about them. Every time he'd send me snail mail, like a check or whatever, there would be an alien drawn on the back and, on the bottom, he'd write "TOP SECRET!" Nick did all kinds of strange shit to get a rise out of you. We'd be talking about a tour or some clinics and all of a sudden be in a conversation about aliens, nothing relevant to what we were talking about a second before. Nick would like to test you. Just to see if you were up—to get your opinion; to see your reaction. That's how he was, brilliant, hilarious, and so plugged in to possibilities.

You'll believe what you will. I can't change you, and I don't want to. You can research everything yourself, assuming the internet exists, of course, and is not just another channel we have here in the Matrix. I'm not here to influence or convince you of anything except that the most dangerous thing the government could possibly want for us is to not question anything.

And so, right after I have dinner, delivered by a Grey alien disguised as a Chinese-food delivery dude, I'm going to record a single by me and Elvis doing our tribute to Paul McCartney, who died in a car crash in the sixties. While he was on his way to an Illuminati meeting.

Time to kiss your family goodnight and marry the dog, dude, because this is it!

Think!

HIT REWIND!

Have you ever thought, "If I could just rewind, man, if I could just rewind?"

Each of our lives can change in an instant, for better or worse. Win the lottery, or never be whole again. One of the worst times of my life had nothing at all to do with music, yet it nearly ended my music career. I still go through some pretty heavy mental torture and anguish just thinking about it. Recalling the story is no easy thing.

(If I could just rewind, man.)

In early 2007, I was helping tear down a wall and was reaching up high over my head with a circular saw. I knew what I was doing. I have a lot of experience in construction and carpentry. I've always enjoyed building decks and helping friends and family with projects like that. I knew how dangerous it could be, but I never thought anything would happen. I locked open the safety guard on the saw, which had been getting in the way and pissing me off. The saw caught on something, kicked back, and snapped right into my left arm above my elbow.

I didn't feel panic or even pain. It was a truly surreal experience, not a drop of blood. That was the bizarre thing. The blade missed every vein and artery. I should have been awash in a gory sea of red but wasn't. Not to say that all these torn folds of flesh and white, fatty tissue and bits of muscle blooming out like some kind of flower wasn't gross. It was heinous. The dude I was with freaked out. He called 911 but I asked him to drive me instead. His fucking car wouldn't start. I'm lucky I hadn't severed an artery, because I would have bled out by the time the paramedics got there forty-five minutes later. They took their sweet-ass time.

It was gnarly. Just thinking about it now makes my arm ache.

After I was stitched up and I knew I was going to be ok, the pain hit, and it hit hard.

If there was even the smallest parting of those dark clouds it was that I hadn't put a fresh, sharp blade on the saw that afternoon. Were it not dull, it might not have caught on something in the wall; were it not dull it would have hot-blade-through-butter taken my arm off.

Maybe the doctors told me that I had a hairline bone fracture, but I didn't hear them if they did. A week, maybe ten days later, I was over at my Mom's place, moving some stuff around in the back yard, trying to keep busy and not feel sorry for myself. Day-dreamingly avoiding my self-pity, I tripped. No big deal, except I landed on my badly injured arm. Clean break right at the fracture. What a fucking knucklehead.

After I had the surgery and the most annoying cast in history was put on my arm, I had a follow up with the specialist.

"When do you think I can play drums?" I asked.

"You play drums?"

"Yeah, that's what I do for a living."

The doctor shook his head and dropped his eyes as if in a dramatic scene in a soap opera. "That's too bad."

"What the fuck are you saying!"

He tried to calm me down as best he could, realizing he'd said exactly the wrong thing.

"Maybe in a few months, we can start to think about it. We have to let everything heal before we'll know anything."

I've never talked about it publicly, but that was the *low* point for me. It wasn't getting fired from Megadeth or anything else. That was the first really brutal fucking milestone.

It wasn't just a month or two. I spent I don't know how long rarely getting out of bed, wallowing in pain and moaning, "Why, why, why did God let this happen to me?" The itchiness and everything else of the cast drove me even crazier, so I ripped it off and put a sling around my arm instead. That felt so much better. Maybe that helped me snap out of being miserable. I'm not sure who or what or how it happened but I guess I just finally realized that self-pity wasn't taking me anywhere.

"I'm so lucky," I thought one morning. "I can still use my hand. I can still wiggle my fingers."

I sat in bed and made up my mind that there was no way I wasn't going to play the drums again. A few days later I slammed a stick down on the snare and the pain shot through me. "Fuck it!" I thought. "Tune that shit out!"

I made the conscious decision that the pain, the injury, was just not going to be a problem.

A month or so after that, I got a call from a friend asking if I could come in and do a session in Hollywood. No one knew that I'd had the accident. I showed up with my left arm in a sling.

"What makes you think you can play with one arm?" the engineer asked. He was just being honest.

"Because I can," I answered. "How do you think I learned to guzzle Gatorade on stage while I was playing? I don't have to use my left arm."

He believed me.

We were getting some sounds and I was learning the parts when the guitar player from the band arrived.

"What the fuck is this guy doing in here?"

"Chill out, dude," the engineer said. "He's already doing better than the guy you had in here with two arms, so shut the fuck up."

The guitarist was a total prick.

"Look, we're not doing any charity fucking handouts. Get this guy out of here. Get somebody who can use both arms!"

He stormed out.

I was pretty bummed and said to the engineer, "Wow. Am I really blowing it?"

He said, "No way, man. Let's have a go at this."

About an hour later, he rang up the guitar player and said, "Check this out, we got it! Oh, yeah, I got rid of that guy with one arm. I got the guy from Megadeth!"

"No way!" the guitarist said. "You got the Megadeth dude! I'm coming right down."

"Nah, he's gone. Came in, did one take and left."

I heard later that the band, no one I want to give any publicity to, loved what I'd done. It was really easy shit, as it turned out, and I nailed it. I asked the engineer if he'd told the guys.

"I didn't have the heart," he said.

It didn't take much longer for me to condition myself back to the level I'd been at before the accident. I still get some phantom psychological pain when I think about how nasty it was.

I've still got the plate and the screws in there. The doctors said it was temporary, that they wanted to go in there to remove them, but they don't bother me. I'm so fearful of another operation and that if it doesn't go right I won't able to play the drums again. I'll leave well enough alone.

Every time I think I know better about something, I look up on the wall of my studio, where I hung that dull saw blade. It's framed with heinous x-rays of my arm. I keep it around just in case some day they need to scrape my DNA off the blade and clone me.

One obnoxious plate and six surgical steel screws later I'm heavy metal for centuries. Dude, I want them to take my conscious awareness and put it into a robo-body. I'll be playing drums until they outlaw it. I'll be robo-dude. I'm going to be the first drummer to jam in space.

CHAPTER NINE

HITTING THINGS WITH STICKS

Here's the coolest thing: My boys Nicholas and Donte still believe in magic, just like their Dad.

"Dad, the Elves won again!"

"Right on, guys! Cool! The Elves are always going to win!"

This makes me so happy because if you stop believing in magic, it stops existing. I've always believed there's magic in everything if you allow it to be.

I see it every day, people who've lost sight of magic or forget about it as they get older. I tell my kids that you've got to dream and have dreams to aspire to fulfill. Dude, I'm still trying to do that. Part of the secret is perspective. I tell people that I was in cryogenics for the past fifteen years. I just came out of a deep freeze, and it's time to shred! When I look back on it, which I've been forced to do working on this book, it just seems as if I've been kind of retired, or on an extended sabbatical. I took ten or twelve years off to help raise my boys. That's a full-time gig right there, a 24/7 job. I love my kids to death. They're like black-ops leaders with too much time on their hands, and I love every second of it. Now that they're a little older, music can again play a larger role in my life—and Nicholas and Donte's as well.

I got back in the groove by playing for at least two hours a day, doing a bunch of play-through drum videos for YouTube playing some of my favorite songs. It's fun, and the fans seem to dig it. If they didn't, I'd know I was blowing it.

I get a lot of calls from new heavy metal bands, and, while it's flattering, it's just not very motivating for me.

Robert Bolger:
I've been working in the music industry for years as an A&R rep and artist management, and I was a huge fan of Megadeth and Nick's drumming. We met years ago, briefly, in the mid-'90s when I was living in L.A. I always thought about Nick and wondered what happened to him when he left Megadeth. Then in 2013, I saw a YouTube video of Nick whaling out to "Holy Wars" and was like, "Holy shit, this dude's still got the fire after all these years!" I contacted Soultone and got Nick a gig playing on a song called "Insolent Scum" for a band I manage called Sufosia. Nick and I then started talking a lot via text and formed a friendship that finally led to me getting him some further session work and some drum clinics. He was reluctant to sign on with a new manager and seemed happy to just do his own thing. But as he started to embrace social media, tens of thousands of fans all over the world began bombarding him with questions, especially about getting back with Mustaine, Junior, and Marty. I had the idea that if there was nothing coming from Mustaine's camp, Nick should form a band with some of the ex-Megadeth members. I figured Nick's fans, and fans of earlier incarnations of Megadeth, would come out in huge numbers to see them play. As always, Nick said, "Ball's in your court, dude. I'm down for whatever." I called Chris Poland and reconnected him and Nick, and then I got James LoMenzo on board to give the trio a chance. The three of them got together for some rehearsals and started recording a few Metallica covers for fun and did a bunch of interviews. When word got out, I started getting tour offers from booking agents from Central America, South America, and all over Europe for the band to tour

as a tribute act. There was a lot of money in the offing. But when it started turning into a "tribute" to themselves, Nick and Chris backed off; they were more focused on writing their own music. Nick joined Chris' band Ohm, and LoMenzo went back to playing bass for John Fogerty. They all had a blast, but it just wasn't meant to be. Just like the Rust In Peace lineup reunion. Nick was the beating heart of Megadeth. He was a huge part of the band's imagery, energy, power, and success.

I'd be into some session work probably, for them, but what I've really wanted to do for the past couple of years (what I've started doing) is hooking up with the players I always wanted to play with. I want to do something reputable. There's been so much that isn't—like these Metal All-Star tours. It sucks when I sign up for something that falls apart or was bogus from the start to take advantage of fans. People think that I've bailed because I wasn't getting my way or getting enough money. Like what happened with the "Metal All-Stars" tour in 2013. I was bummed at first, and it blew when I found out they'd fucked up with the money. But it was way deeper than that. Turns out some of the stars they'd advertised on the tour had never agreed, or in some cases had never even been approached. They were just using the names to sell bogus tickets. At first, it seemed like a no-brainer. Me, Tom Araya, Vince Neil, Philip Anselmo, Joey Belladonna, Zakk Wylde, Udo Dirkschneider, Cronos, Max Cavalera, Brian Fair, Matt Bachand and Jon Donais, and former Manowar member Ross the Boss. Rob, my manager, called me the day before I was supposed to fly out and said, "Dude, you're not going."

At first, I was pissed. Great management, Rob, can we do that again? But it wasn't Rob's fault. He did everything he could to make it happen. When I first signed on, I was stoked. Going to Russia and all over Europe and South America sounded rad to me, but the more I learned, the lamer it sounded. When they told me that I'd be doing a Manowar song, "Kings of Metal," I was, like, "No, dude. I'm not getting baby-oiled up and putting on a fucking furry loincloth."

Fuck that, kiddies.

Me, James LoMenzo, and Chris Poland.

Age is just a number, and my number is fifty-one. I am Area 51. I can play anything, but I don't have that burning desire to go out and play stadiums all over the world for 300 nights a year any more. One tour? I'd do it. I have come to value home and family and, truth be told, more musical challenges.

Before the last Megadeth reunion attempt, I had teamed up with Chris Poland and James LoMenzo for what journalists started calling a "supergroup," since we were three ex-Megadeth players. My manager Rob got the three of us together, and it was a great idea. We rehearsed quite a bit, getting to know each other musically since we were never in Megadeth at the same time. We did some radio and internet publicity together and truly had a blast. We went through a lot of old videotape and recordings of us at various stages in our individual Megadeth careers. I was impressed playing together. I mean, I've been a fan of both these guys for a long time. It's not just mutual admiration—the three of us share a musical language. We did a cover of Metallica's "Motorbreath" and put it out on YouTube just to stoke everyone's fire.

It's great to play all those old those songs, and a bunch of Zeppelin, when you're working on your chops or just for fun, but after a few months of rehearsing I realized that it's not what I want to do musically. For me, if it doesn't excite me, it's not where I want to be.

My manager thought it would be a cool Megadeth tribute thing, and that's when I realized what it was turning into. I'm not doing a tribute to myself; I don't care how much money is in it. I wouldn't feel good about it. It's kind of blasphemous. Chris said the same thing.

As for James, he's an awesome player and a no-holds-barred working musician. The project wasn't what he was looking for, either. I don't think any of us regret trying. James went back to supporting John Fogerty on the road, while I had what I think is one of the greatest good fortunes of my life with Chris' invitation to join his fusion band Ohm, with Robertino "Pag" Pagliari.

Chris and Pag have had Ohm going on since about 2002, and I've been hanging around them for years, just not playing with them. When their drummer, David Eagle, had a heart attack and was in the hospital for surgery, Chris asked me to join them for a benefit concert for him. Of course, I was in. He sent me about a dozen songs. I called him back and said, "Dude, I don't know if I'm good enough to play with you guys. This music is really technical. There's a lot of different changes, a lot of information to learn at one time, and I don't know if I can do it."

Chris laughed. "Of course you can," he said.

It was a total mindfuck, trying to play exactly what David was playing. It was a merry-go-round in my head, and it wasn't good. David's style was radically different than mine. He's really musical, where I'm a lot heavier and into driving the band. I met David once, at NAAM the previous year, and he was really cool. When I started rehearsing for the benefit gig, he wrote me from the hospital. "Don't try to be David Eagle, be Nick Menza." That was really awesome because, out of respect, I wanted to play just like he did.

I listened to the whole catalogue and listened to the songs I played naturally and came up with a list for Chris and Pag. They showed me what they had, and the next thing you knew we had fifteen songs. Once they were locked in, I had three weeks to learn them inside out. I did nothing else right up until the day of the show. I was practicing when my tech came to the door. I was sweating, my hair was all wet, I was in shorts, and I had a towel around my neck.

"Dude! What are you doing?"

"What are you talking about? I'm practicing."

"We have to be at the Baked Potato! You're on in like fifteen minutes."

I'm all, "Cool. I just gotta check out this one part."

I started walking back to my drum room, and he grabbed my snare and stick bag and said, "We gotta go *now!*"

"Ok, ok, chill out bro. Here, put this in your car."

I gave him a CD of the music to listen to on the way over, and I played on the dashboard while he drove. I was nervous, dude.

The Baked Potato is tiny and holds only about eighty people. It's really intimate—people standing up at the bar, the tables right up close—and hot as fuck. When I'm up there, it's like I'm sweating into people's food. You're under the microscope in that kind of situation. Ohm's sound is really clean. It's loud, but a whole different vibe for me, not a theatrical thing where you're hamming out, pointing at the exit signs with your sticks and stuff. I'm happy to be featured in an upcoming documentary, *The Passion of the Potato*, about the awesome legacy of the Baked Potato that some cool filmmakers, James Smith, Madison Koronez, and Debra Smith are making. We've been shooting stuff for about a year, and it's going to be really cool. It was the perfect place for us to start out because the band is about the music, and the fans who come to the Baked Potato are mostly musicians themselves. I work well under pressure like that. Dude, you get one crack at that, and you don't get to rewind.

When it was over I told the guys I thought I sucked. Pag and Chris told me it was great and that I pulled it off. I wasn't perfect, but we did it, and the crowd loved it. It was a great tribute to David, which was the point. The show wasn't about me or Chris or Pag.

It was so tragic when, a couple of weeks later, David died. It was fucked up. Rest in peace, my drum brother.

The week after David died, Chris and Pag and I were together again talking about the future of the band. That's when they asked me to join. I knew I wanted to do it, but my head was swimming.

Then when I went into the rehearsal room and started setting my kit up where David's kit had been, I felt a vibe in the room—a really good vibe. I told Pag I had a weird feeling, and he said he did too. David was there. I think you hang around after you die. I'm sure you linger and look at your life. I'm sure it's part of your growth as you move onto the next dimension—the next life that we take from here, the energy and everything. I don't think we just turn off.

There are memories, love and family and all those things that you hold onto in this world before it's time to move on. It's hard to describe, but it felt right.

Ohm is a whole other animal from anything I've ever encountered. Pag plays all these melodies on the bass while Chris is playing another melody, and the drums are yet another part. If you were to listen to each instrument individually, you wouldn't think we were playing the same song; the song is an invisible fourth element that comes out of the three of us. It's not easy to describe. The closest I can say for someone who's never heard us is that there's a Rush vibe, but it's cleaner and more sophisticated.

Chris' Jeff Beck influences shine through. We were talking briefly about bringing Rusty Cooley into the band on second guitar. Rusty is super cool. I really got into his seven-string playing, and he's really challenged me as a songwriter, inspiring me to tackle some pretty high musical rungs like Fredrik Thordendal and Mårten Hagström of Meshuggah, when it comes to my own solo stuff.

We also talked about getting a vocalist, but honestly, Chris' guitar playing *is* the singer. There are areas in the songs where it's pure musical invention and exploration. Each of us really has to know where to come out of the breaks, and it's truly challenging. That's one of the most exciting things about playing with these guys.

I turned my favorite producer, Max Norman, onto what we're doing, because this fusion stuff is his favorite kind of music. Branching into more sophisticated, refined music is the natural progression of things for most musicians.

You just don't play metal drums at fifty or sixty-years-old. There are guys who are in their twenties running circles around you, no matter how good you are or were. You're just not going to play like you did when you were twenty—you're going to play like you're fifty! There's less energy. I am absolutely a better drummer now than I was when I was twenty, but at that age I didn't need to build myself up into a machine to play like I did every night; I was already there.

Jazz or fusion, obviously, is way different than playing metal. But in anything I play, you can hear the metal because I'm a heavy player, and I make the music that way, period. I could be playing for Katy Perry, and it's going to be heavy. I can play any style of music, but when it really comes down to it when I step out to play live, I play the way Nick Menza does. That's my style, and it's always going to come through no matter what the music is.

It's about the sound with this band, the intricacies and interplays. I'm trying to get my sound refined for them. In turn, they've changed how they play. There are some songs the two of them have been playing for ten or fifteen years now, but even those have taken on a whole new dynamic just because there's a new equation now.

David was counterpoint on everything, never playing the same beat that Chris and Pag were playing. He got in between it and around it. Now the band has a different sound because it's a different drummer. We are a lot more syncopated than they were before. I play it like Bonham would have played it. Overall, it's less jazzy, but for the first time in my life I am trying to bring some Buddy Rich into my mix. Dude, that's totally the beat you have to lay in there. A six-eight beat. One of those feels. I straightened it right out, and now it sounds like a rock ballad, with a bit of Buddy. It's the Menza for the New Century.

We played a metal festival, and the security guards were all these gangbangers, into hip-hop and rap and R&B shit. They were totally tripping on us because, as a jazzy rock fusion band, we were the only band there that had any differential from these death metal bands. Our security guards were checking it out, hanging out in our room, these white guys playing this shit. "Dude! That was awesome, you guys really rock."

We have a couple of high-energy tunes that are just over-the-top. When we play them, I feel like I'm barely holding on, looking at Pag as we play. Pag is unreal. He's one of the sickest bass players I've ever played with. Robertino Pagliari—a totally underrated musician. He won't play with frets. He's got an absolutely unique style and sound. He can play anything. He slides around, bending harmonics and stuff. I don't know how he does it. And his bass weighs a hundred pounds or something. If you let go of the bass, the neck will hit the floor. I pick it up and it's like, "Dude! No wonder your back is fucked up. You should have this thing on a stand with wheels."

We'll make a seriously awesome record. When I first started jamming with them, they said I needed to play more. And they didn't mean rehearsing; they meant in the songs. "Go off, dude, go nuts. Play whatever you want. Play anything, whatever excites you. You need to play *more*. Crazy out of control. Go off!"

It's free and open, you can stop playing, but you have to know where to come back or the whole thing falls apart. The three of us have telepathy, and the two of them, having played together for like fifteen years, have awesome little hand signals they do to each other; I'm starting to read that stuff.

We record everything when we're jamming so we don't forget any of the cool stuff we come up with. Start with one riff, and who knows where it ends up. It's cool for me to be playing music like that instead of written, structured stuff.

People really get off with us. It's the musician factor of Chris and Pag that's the big sell factor. The right people have to hear us. If we get in the right places and certain circles, it's going to be all over. This band's going to be huge. It's the dream band for me. I've been casually working with Polish guitarist Widek and Symphony X bassist Mike LePond and Threat Signal front man Jon Howard on the band for my Atomic Disintegrator animation project, but I'm putting it and everything else on hold.

You can't be in a band with Chris and Pag and expect it to be a part-time gig. I'll still do sessions if I'm really into them, but I'm putting my total focus on Ohm. This is the band I've been looking for forever.

Ohm, with Robertino "Pag" Pagliari and Chris Poland.

I'd like to call it my "dream gig." But, well, my "dream gig" would have to be with my Dad.

"Dad, you write all the tunes, and I'll just play drums."

That would be my ultimate dream, to do a record with him—Dad writing all the songs and coming up with all the ideas. It wouldn't matter what kind of music it is. It could be jazz or whatever, just for me to write some drum features in there and have him play sax and some solos. We'll just burn it down, dude. No vocals; no bullshit. No guitar. My Dad's not big on guitar players. He's from the big band era. It's hard to have piano and guitar together and keep them in tune, and he's a real stickler for that shit.

He's pretty hip. He's played with huge people, and he's still playing. He's never retiring, and neither am I. Music is a way of life and way of making a living at living life. And just like life, quitting music is about as natural to me as stopping breathing.

I hope I die on my drum set.

SOAP IN MY EYES

It's funny, the questions I get asked by fans. Whether I'm meeting them on the street or backstage, it's never boring. The kids are obviously interested, and, dude, I'm a fan, too. *What's it like to be a rock star? What's it like to play in front of hundreds of thousands of people?* People ask stuff about sex and drugs and life on the road, which are always to be expected. But you know the one question I think I'm asked more than any other, especially by drummers or kids who want to be rock drummers?

What hair product do you use?

Really! At first, I thought it was just about the stupidest question possible. Then I realized it's probably the smartest from kids who dream of being on stage themselves. I figured that out when I started answering people completely honestly, without making a wisecrack about it. On nights when I'm out on the road and playing, the answer is *none*. True. And that was a lesson learned early on the hard way. Playing the way I always have, and especially in a band like Megadeth, you're breaking into a soaking-wet sweat by the time you're two songs in. You can't have hair products or stuff dripping down your forehead into your eyes. That shit stings! I mean, I'd love to tell you I use some high-end and obscenely expensive hair products with the hope I land a cool endorsement deal and get a carton of shit for free in the mail, but the truth is I try to go easy on all that stuff. I just keep my hair clean and completely product-free on nights I'm performing.

And, now, I want to share with you the best moment I ever had with you fans while playing with Megadeth. It was in Tasmania, and there were all these kids in wheelchairs in a special VIP stand. They were able to wheel themselves down to the stage do stage dives and then get passed around and back into their chairs. Man, it was ballsy! I so respected the promoters and everybody for making this possible for these kids, and that night they showed *us* what was real rock 'n' roll spirit. I'll never forget that sight and that feeling.

Thank *you*, dudes!

CHAPTER TEN

DRUM WORSHIP

How is a drum solo like a sneeze? You can tell it's coming, but you can't do anything about it. Another old music joke, but, like most jokes, it's centered on some truth.

I used to get asked that all the time. "Dude! Why don't you do solos?" The answer to that is pretty simple: if you have chops, show them off in the first few seconds of the first song. Unless you're Buddy Rich or Neil Peart (and you're not) I want to hear what you can do in a song; I don't want to hear you wank off playing a solo. Big deal, you can play really fast; you can play really hard.

In my first bands, starting out and competing in the ruthless L.A. club scene, I played a lot of solos, and we always played *really* loud. We got in trouble pretty much every time we played, since we'd crank the volume way higher than we had played at soundcheck.

We had to because we were in the death match of our lives to stand out against the million other bands. Part of that, in the day, was to demolish the place with a drum solo. It was great for winding the crowd up and over the top.

As I became a better drummer and matured, I settled into being as serious as I can about the music, not the flash. Once I joined Megadeth and started playing that kind of music, a solo would be anti-climactic. I play in a hammering style all the time. I don't play with brushes. I play to sweat, man! Any drummer in any heavy metal band is working from beginning to end. That's why you play drums in a band like that—because that's how you want to play. You don't want to be kicking back, prancing along. I could get into something cohesive that might get the crowd going, but, truthfully, I have always believed that an audience would rather hear another song by the band.

I've started doing drum clinics all over the place (I seem to still be particularly popular in Mexico and South America, which is cool) and have been recording my first instructional DVD, so I've been putting a lot of thought into what I think every drummer should hear just as he or she is starting out. No matter what genre of music you might be into, this is an ultimate "crash" course in all the basics you need to know. Pay attention, and you may never crack a cymbal or break a stick again. You'll get the best possible sound out of whatever kit you own, and, I'll tell you what you need to know about tuning your set and setting up your cymbals.

Hi, my name is Nick, and I hit things with sticks.

I'm glad you've made it this far, because this is what I think is the most important part of the book. I'm in the mood to tell you some secrets. I'm not worried about giving them away because you'll never be able to do exactly what I do on a drum kit just, as I will never be able to do exactly what you do! We could be on identical kits with identical sticks playing exactly the same thing, and it's not going to sound the same—similar maybe, but not the same.

It's just like guitar players playing the favorite riffs of their heroes never sound exactly the same because music is human, and we're all different, endlessly variable and unique. No one's going to apply exactly the same pressure on a guitar string. And no one's going to apply the same pressure, if you will, to a drum kit.

We all explore other drummers' styles. At first, I soaked up every song I could by John Bonham and Neil Peart. I learned all the parts and developed the technical chops. And I learned that there is a *feeling* to great drumming that you either have or you don't, and that this *feeling* is where your individual style comes from, in time. The more you practice, the more you learn the basic vocabulary of drumming and build your own vocabulary within your capabilities as a player.

Everyone is different. I can't honestly say you would be better not getting lessons. Or whether lessons would be crucial to your development. We're all different. Lessons were not for me. I learned by listening, watching, and doing.

My dad offered to send me to the best schools for music, but I knew that wasn't the right path for me. I learned a lot from the drummers my Dad played with. These guys were often at our house, and I can only begin to tell you the awesome things I soaked up from them. Steve Gadd was incredible to me (and broke my bass drum playing my kit once!). Chuck Flores showed me some trippy hand exercises. Louie Bellson sent me my first double-bass drum kit as a gift when I was a teenager. Joe Porcaro was really nice to me, but he was old school and told me I wasn't holding my sticks the right way, that I needed to start my training over again. That wasn't going to work for me. I am too impatient for that! I wanted to play, not take lessons!

I believe in doing whatever works for you. If it's formal lessons that set you on the right path, go for it. If you need to find that path on your own, go for it.

I'm a Neanderthal drummer. I play loud and hard. I try to break things! For me, and the style of drumming I do, it's about pressure. Every hit counts. It's not like one of those things where you're kicking back, relaxing, and playing along. It's about pressure applied and volume.

Just because I didn't take formal lessons doesn't mean I didn't have an education or teachers. The best teacher was Buddy Rich. No one could touch that guy. Buddy could things that other drummers just aren't capable of doing. He was the master of the drums. He could do rolls on the snare that sounded like air compressors. He could do it really loud or really soft. He was ferocious. Just like my Dad on the tenor sax; he's ferocious when he wants to be. To this day I've never seen a drummer who even comes close to him. You don't have to like jazz. Watch all the

Buddy Rich you can on YouTube. There are a lot of amazing drummers out there, but he was the greatest drummer on the planet. I got so many lessons just by hanging around and watching him.

I listened to all the big-band stuff because they were the masters, and that's what my Dad plays. I've always heard that the best composers don't borrow; they steal! It's all been done before. Your job is to find a new way of doing the same things. It's all in the presentation and feel. The trick is to grab all these tricks and licks and beats from your favorite drummers, put them in your little bag, and take it to the next level—make it your own. Develop your own style and your own identity with the way you set your drums up and the way people perceive you: the theatrical art of drumming. There are thousands of people who play amazingly, but when they play they don't move an inch. The viewers are baffled because it doesn't look like it sounds on the record. The visual doesn't match the sound. It's important for drummers to have an identity, a look, and a cool setup. I always looked first for the drum kit when I went to concerts. I loved when it was hidden behind a curtain, and I'd be sitting there stoked on for the first couple of songs, so I could look at all the equipment, the hardware, how it was set up. I had a few lessons from some really important influences, but mostly I learned to play by putting on headphones and playing along to records.

I'm basically a feel-style drummer. I play by feel. I don't know how to read music well. I understand the breakdowns of time signatures, but I didn't practice any rudiments growing up, doing rolls and five-stroke rolls, paradiddles and all that shit. If I did, I did without knowing it. I'm a single-stroke dude. I don't do doubles because it's just not as powerful as single strokes. You can learn to accent single strokes the same way you do double strokes. I keep getting asked about my technique, and I say, "What technique!" Sometimes I hold the stick in my hand like a baseball bat just so I know it's not going to fly out of my hand when I stand up to hit a cymbal.

Neil Peart always had a great setup and a great style. I know pretty much every Rush song on the drums. I used to look inside their records just to see what kind of equipment they were using, what his setup was like, what heads he was using, what sticks, and any changes to his setup from the previous record and tour.

One time I happened to be in Phoenix on tour at the same time as Rush, on one of our "non-performance" days. I went backstage after the show hoping to meet Neil. Sadly, it was around the time he was going through some tragic personal stuff, and he had gone straight from the stage onto his bus.

I knew his tech, Larry, and I asked him if he would ask Neil to sign a copy of that month's *Modern Drummer* magazine, as Neil was on the cover and there was an interview with me inside.

Larry came back with my magazine. Neil had written, "To Nick, happy drumming (Mega-Life!) Neil Peart." At first, I was like, *Whoa! That's kinda weird. Is he dissing me or the band?*

I was actually nervous to meet him. I still hope to one day shake Neil's hand, because he is one of my all-time favorite drummers, and I've been so fortunate to meet and get to know just about every one of my heroes. Now that he's retired and lives near me, maybe we'll cross paths again. He definitely influenced me in a huge way, showing me the limitless possibilities of percussion. His whole style is a perfect alchemy of every drummer who's come before him. Neil's a great lyricist and a great drummer, with a tremendous theatrical approach. He's truly the Professor of the Drum Kit!

When Jeff and I were trying to think of a title for this book, I told him the story, and he said, "That's it! *Megalife!*" I told him I didn't know, because Junior's church or ministry is called "Mega Life Ministries."

"We're not putting out a ministry," Jeff said. "We're putting out a book, and Neil's the one who gave you the title."

Tommy Aldridge is another hero of mine. He was clearly inspired by some of the same jazz players as I was, like Joe Morello and Louis Bellson, especially the double-kick thing. Bellson had the vision for double bass, and Tommy came along and brought it to rock 'n' roll for all of us. They were the pioneers. When you watch Tommy, he's not playing; he's attacking the drum kit. He plays with big sticks and plays the style I love. You

want a rock drummer? Get Tommy Aldridge. He'll light up your music for you.

My DVD is in the process of being edited. We shot with six cameras all around me as I talk about the pedals and heads I use, and why I play the style I do. I'm trying to make it interactive where you can switch between cameras. I'm going to offer a sound library, too, so you can change the sounds. There will be a loops library that you can use if you want to have Nick Menza on your album.

It's going to have about ten songs on it. I recorded fourteen tracks, all Megadeth. I'd love to do all kinds of my original shit, maybe even some rad covers, but the truth is that ever since I left Megadeth the fans have never stopped being on me. "You've got to get back with Megadeth. You've got to get back in the band." I'm not going to argue. It's what they love, and it's what they want to hear and learn how to play on drums, the way I played it. So I'm going to give it to them.

It's going to be a really cool package, not just video of me drumming. It will have information about heads and drum configurations. I want to share what I've learned. It's all about feel! Does it feel right to you? Are you acting on your highest level of joy and excitement? If you're acting on that level, then you're going to be successful at anything you do.

I know a lot of guys who do stuff they don't want to do just to get paid. It's not their highest level of excitement, and it shows through. People have asked me, "How did you get to be *that guy*?" You've got to do what excites you the most. Then you'll never really work a day in your life, because you'll be doing what you love.

Is there a right way to do stuff? Not always. Right now, I'm using cymbals for crashes that say "ride" on them. It's all about what you want to hear. It doesn't matter to me whether it says "Latin series" or "vintage" or "gospel." I have a couple of cymbals from every line in my family of sounds. I've customized a couple of them by taking a grinder to them. It opens them up and makes them more "rock" sounding. I've got a new signature line at Soultone, the last of the great cymbal makers from Turkey making cymbals by hand. A lot of the cymbal makers these days make millions of cymbals by machine. I don't think they even listen to what they sound like before they get their stamp on them, wrap them up, and send them out to the shops—they sound so lame. I want my cymbals to sound like the sun god, Ra.

I have never, since they started in 2005, cracked one Soultone cymbal. I broke many Zildjians over the years, and my style of playing hasn't changed at all. I like the loudest, largest cymbals I can use. One trick is to not use the wing nuts on the cymbals on the stands, because that's where you can crack them—up at the bell. I tell people, "Don't tighten your cymbal down," but they say it's the only way to keep the cymbals from hitting each other. Well, you should think about that when you're cracking cymbals left and right. If I ever break a cymbal, I'll usually break it around the edge of it. I'll crack it from playing through it. But mostly, cymbals get cracked because of lack of technique. If you take a stick and just follow through and bash it as hard as you can, of course you're going to crack any cymbal, and it's not fair to say the cymbal's bad. Every once in a while, you'll get a cymbal with a factory defect, and there will be a nearly invisible crack along the lathing. The Soul-tones are bulletproof if you play properly.

Specifically, I use sixteen-inch hats. They're custom Soultones that were actually symphony cymbals that you're supposed to hold in your hands. I saw them in the shop and went "Yeah!" Everyone laughed at me and said I couldn't use sixteens, but I do. I have used them since 2005. These are the same exact cymbals I've been using for over ten years. That's how awesome they are. I've never found a better-sounding set of high hats, so I hope I never break them or crack them. I take them every-where I go, every session I play—same with my rides. My main right now is a twenty-four-inch Extreme Ride. I've got a couple of smaller ones as well. A twenty-two-inch Natural Crash Ride and a twenty-inch Bril-liant Ride, the same rides I got back in 2005. I slam on those. I play on the bell with the butt end of the sticks. I pound on them. I do my own hammering as I play! For crashes, I'm using two nineteen-inch Extreme Brilliant Crashes and two twenty-inch Brilliant Crashes.

As for drums, I play the DC California kits exclusively. I always check out other cymbals and drums because I want my sound to be as good as I can make it, but I haven't found anything better than those two prod-ucts. I must have ten full kits collecting dust out in my garage that I've had for decades and never use. They're great kits, but they don't sound as good as these DC California's and Soultones.

The most important thing I can tell you is that you need dope equip-ment. This may sound obvious and might be a real downer, since great equipment is going to set you (or your parents!) back a good 6,000 to 15,000 dollars for the drums, hardware, and cymbals.

While the marquee drums I favor are DC California, it's pretty hard to go wrong with a good set of DW. They're among the most popular and highest-quality drums being made today. So are Sonar. Basically, any of the major brand's top-of-the-line kits are going to sound good. Sure, you can go cheaper with a Guitar Center set of Ludwigs, Pearls, Tama, or Yamaha for a few hundred bucks on the low end, but if you can't go all out, at least plunk down a grand and get a good Gretsch kit. A simi-larly priced Sonar kit isn't going to let you down, either. You get what you pay for. Get the heaviest hardware you can afford. When it comes to cymbals, Soultone are the only ones I use or recommend. They're the best. What's more is that you can get a basic set as low as five hundred to one thousand dollars.

Vintage cymbals from the '60s and now '70s are out there, but, like anything, you have to truly know what you're doing to not get ripped off.

Your favorite drummer is endorsing one drum line and one cymbal line. Just know that the gear he's using isn't something you can pick up at your local store.

Most of us use custom-made lines to our own specifications. You're going to pay handsomely for those. Neil Peart's DW kit is not something you can walk into a store and buy, although you *can* buy one of the few exact replicas that the company built at the same time it made Neil's last set if you have an extra thirty thousand dollars sitting around.

As for the standard off-the-shelf cymbals, Sabien, Paiste and Zildjian (in that order)—they're all companies that you can find pretty decent cymbals from, but they're machine-stamped and you really have to go through them carefully to get something that doesn't sound lame.

Now for some basics: the bigger the cymbal, the easier it is to crack. That's because the thicker they are, the shockwaves don't have anywhere to go. If they're really thin, they're going to bend and absorb the impact. Now, I always prefer the big crash rides for that Bonham sound. You hit it hard and it opens up, and when you don't hit hard it just rings beautifully. It will take you a long time to learn how to hit cymbals properly. Don't just bash away. They'll sound like shit, or you'll crack them. You've got to learn how to swipe them, smack them to the side, and bounce the stick off when you hit them. If you just follow through and play as hard as I do, you're likely to crack even the best cymbals.

However you go, you've got to spend at least 2,500 dollars *minimum* to get a basic kit with hardware and cymbals before you're going to have something truly worthy of learning on. I'll tell you this: you're only going to sound as good as your gear. Take that to the bank. You have to get the best equipment you can afford to sound the best you can!

I told you about my cymbals. Here's my rig rundown, which hasn't changed much in a few years now. My drums, except for the snare, are all DC California shells.

For the bass drums, I use two 24x18 shells (unless I'm using two pedals), Evans single-coated and Remo Power Stroke heads. I use double-bass, of course, everywhere I can, but sometimes that's just not feasible, in which case I use two pedals. For my toms, I have twelve-inch, thirteen-inch, fourteen-inch mounted and eighteen-inch and twenty-inch floor toms. I use Emperor coated or Remo Black Suede heads up top and clear Ambassadors on the bottom.

Now, for snares! I am a total Snare Snob. I generally don't use anything off the rack, unless it's *my* rack! My snares are all custom shells. My favorite is actually one I made out of a brass sewer pipe. Most of the time I'm using an 8x14-inch, free-floating with Pearl hardware. I also use a sixteen-inch by six-and-a-half-inch Mahogany eight-ply and a fourteen-inch by eight-inch brass-hammered snare that I have very tight.

I've always wondered why they don't make drum heads out of Kevlar. I mean, if you can't put a bullet through it, how are you going to put a beater or stick through it? I know, companies make money by selling drumhead after drumhead, but why not charge two hundred dollars per head instead? Make the same amount of money, but then you don't have replace them once a week if you're on the road. When I'm out on a world tour, I'd put Kevlar patches on mine. For one whole Megadeth tour, I went without having to replace my snare or bass heads.

Triggers are not something you're likely to get into for a few years, but I think they're a must-have for your live metal sound. But only live! In the studio, I am the drummer!

Same deal with click tracks, which can be a tricky proposition. It depends on what you're recording. If you want the band to sound live, a click will turn you into robots, but if you want or need absolute perfect meter, there's nothing better. I've always found them easy to play with but troublesome because I need the click as loud as I can get it in my headphones; and when I do, there's a risk of it bleeding into the overhead microphones. Ultimately, they're incredibly helpful, especially if you have trouble with meter. Still, I prefer the raw sound and feel of not using one. As energy builds and the excitement mounts, players tend to speed up. It's natural. I like that! If there's a single difference between *Rust In Peace* and *Countdown To Extinction*, it's that *RIP* was recorded live and *Countdown* was done to a click. Using the click puts your brain governor on, which only lets you break out into a certain energy field, where you can't get crazy the way you would live. If you play to a click, it's done. You're done. Worst-case is the energy stagnates. If you go in and write the songs on the spot, then you don't really play what occurs naturally, if you play it a thousand times. It's the magic of jamming that gives records the human element, which technology fucks with. Real jamming, when people play together and it's tight, has to fluctuate. We've come so far technologically with sound, but everyone has the same sound. There's less clarity between bands. They've got the same sounds, huge drums, huge bass, and huge production. To me, it's lacking the song content that comes from guys playing in a room together at the same time. In the studio, stuff occurs naturally. The magic happens. Most bands these days don't have that. I call them virtual bands because they're sending files back and forth via computers. When I hear that kind of music, I go, "Next song. Next band."

You need that live energy. The drummer's driving the tank. In heavy rock bands, if the drummer's not on top of it, there's no energy and drive playing to the riffs. You've got to play to the beat or a little ahead of it.

Tuning drums is a workshop in itself, but here's the basic routine I've always used. Some heads, like Remos, have a seal that needs to be broken by tightening. I do this with all my heads. Instead of a key, I use a power drill to initially put the heads on, to make sure they're tight, especially the snare. I start with my floor toms and move up, one hand on the drum and the other tightening each lug as I go around the head counter-clockwise. Not that it makes a difference, of course, but that's the way I do it. Generally, I choose my cymbals so that my cymbal family moves from above my hi-hat down to above my second floor tom in a descending tonal pattern that sounds like a doorbell. I tune my drums the same way, and that's where the key comes in. For the kind of music

I play, drums don't need to be tuned to anything in particular, as long as they're in tune with themselves. Sort of like life.

For pedals, I use flat beaters. Currently I'm using DWs 9000s. But I go to Home Despot (Home Depot) and get bigger, thicker springs because I like them much tighter and stronger than you get them from the factory. I tell guys, it's not about your foot playing every accent, every note, it's the pedal that works for you. If you're using really heavy beaters with the weights up on them like I do, to make them even heavier, with the spring tension just right, I can take my foot off the pedal, and it will bounce on the head a couple of times if I want it to. What your foot does is it stops the pedal from hitting the bass drum again. A lot of times I find myself resting the beater on the head and leaving it there, and hitting it again, because it's going to spring back so hard. You want it to come back; that's what you need the tension for.

When you start playing really fast double-bass stuff, the pedals start working for you, and it's about jockeying them into position and into the tempo of whatever you're playing. I play heel up, always. Some guys do heel down, but you can't get any power that way. I like to throw into the head, and I like a lot of pitch on the beater—have the beaters as far back as they'll go, almost hitting the top of my foot. Some guys play with double pedals rather than double bass, but it all depends on the music you're playing, or the size of the stage or space you're in. Beaters will cancel each other out coming off the drumhead when you're playing fast metal. Without two bass drums, you're going to be getting in your own way.

I'm using custom sticks that are about an inch longer than regular sticks. For ages, I was using the biggest Nightsticks I could find. Think about it: with little sticks, you're using twice the energy that you'd need using big sticks to get the same bang for your effort. Big sticks help do the work for you. When I joined Megadeth, we rehearsed for over a year before we played live. I was shocked to discover (though it makes perfect sense now) you never play as hard in rehearsal as you do on stage, and if you don't have your hands in shape before you go on the road, you are fucked. Your hands are going to be blistered and bleeding and make you miserable, even if you go out with gloves on. And that effects your playing, of course.

With Ohm, I've made some changes. When I started playing with Chris and Pag, I decided to downsize sticks a little for the finesse I need. With every challenge comes necessary change to my equipment and technique. Not to say I sound a lot different. If I were to play nursery rhymes, I'd still bring a whole lotta heavy.

How you hold your sticks is something you'll have to decide for your-self, based on what you play and what's comfortable. There's the "Tradi-tional Grip" or "Matched Stick Grip." This is what you see Buddy Rich and most jazz players (Stewart Copeland or Charlie Watts on the rock side) doing. Then there's what I and most rock and metal drummers do, which is a straight-ahead grip—stick held the same way in both hands. I could never get the power and volume I wanted with the traditional grip. It's up to you, but it's a good idea to learn both.

Here are some secrets when it comes to sticks. When I go on a tour of any length, I file grooves into the stick bottoms for a better grip, and I take the lacquer off to prevent them from slipping and so I won't get blisters. I also pay attention to the grain on each stick. Make sure it's running in one direction, or the stick is pretty much guaranteed to break or splinter. And the fucking things have to be straight! I know how obvious this seems, but I don't play with a stick unless it's passed my "Table Test." It's simple! Take each stick and roll it across a table. If it rolls true, it's straight. If it doesn't, well, it's kindling or a new chew toy for your dog. Generally, I break the tips off and play with the butt ends of the sticks for a fatter sound, because there's simply more stick hitting the head, hence more volume. People ask me how often I use brushes, and the answer is, "All the time. To dust off my cymbals."

It's amazing how differently you can set up a drum kit. I've found that it varies greatly from drummer to drummer. Some dudes set their stuff up in ways that other people find really difficult to play.

I mentioned earlier that I'd set up Buddy's kit up a few times. The way he had his snare tilted worked wonders for Buddy, but I couldn't get into it. I couldn't get any power when I tried it. Every setup is going to be different.

As for my setup, there are a few basics I'd like to share. Overall, it's about the balance point. I sit pretty high up, for instance. Sometimes I stand up to hit a cymbal and step on a pedal and I need that tension, that pressure, to make it work. You need to take the time to experiment and find out what works for you. Change stuff around and see how your body responds. Take it from one end of the spectrum to the other and see what fits. No matter what, make it comfortable.

I set up with plenty of room to move, to stand up; to sweat! It's crucial to stay hydrated if you're playing the kind of sets I did in Megadeth. On a typical night back in those days, I'd go through a gallon of water and a gallon of Gatorade. If you're doing it right, you're in a marathon, and you're in it to win.

I guess I should mention the Greg Voelker Rack that a few of us made famous in the '80s and '90s. Well, that Greg Voelker made famous. Greg's system included a double-bass drum kit with the tom-toms mounted on a lower chrome rack and all crashes mounted on a higher rack that was supported by two chrome bars placed behind the drummer. It was designed for its lack of stands and a riser, which suspends the bass drums, so they float. The flexibility with the design gave me ultimate mounting options, got rid of all the annoying stands and, most importantly, ensured my whole setup was exactly the same every night. (It looked rad, too, and it opened up the sight lines for the audience to see me—and for me to see the audience.)

Think about it in these terms. What if you were a piano player, and every night the keys were in a different place? That's what I was facing every night before I got the Rack. The drums were never precisely the way I wanted them, and I could never count on the cymbals and all the hardware to be my idea of perfect. For that kind of performance, you need perfect, because you need everything possible in your favor to make it to the finish line.

It was awesome for Megadeth, of course, but it was also so heavy, difficult, and expensive to move that it took the road crew of a huge band to make it feasible. Every night, the guys had to move it, load it, and unload it using a lift. It's not the kind of thing you're going to want at home or in the studio. I gave mine up a long time ago, but there was no other way to do what I was doing at the time.

For microphones, I prefer the minimum number possible, kept as far away as possible. Put mics in too close, and they'll always end up needing gates and compressors, which fucks with your natural sound. Just two overheads, one in each kick and one on the snare, and that'll do.

The drums need to be angled only a little bit toward me. Too much angle and I'll damage the heads before I'm half way through a set. The cymbals need to be placed as flat as possible—hence the genius of Greg's Rack: the flatter placement means the cymbals' sound waves are going straight out rather than bouncing all over the place and getting lost. And, dude, you should have stick tubes all over the place. I have them on each side and one in the middle. You're a fucking drummer! When you need a stick you need it *now*!

I always used a huge monitor behind me and to the right so I could hear, or hope to hear, what was going on with the whole band. I never liked in-ear monitors because there's just never enough bass response in them. Bass comes from air movement. You can't get it any other way. It's not about volume; it's about fidelity. Headphones always bleed too much and the way I play, I couldn't have fucking cords draping down my back. Even when I tried taping phones to my head with duct tape they'd fly off because I get so drenched in sweat. That's why I ended up designing my own, which are Sony guts inside industrial, sound-proof safety headphones—zero bleed, all the fidelity *and* volume I want. I call them "EarBombs," or "Ear-Drumz." If I find some investors or discover that there's a market for my design, I'll start my own line of headphones for drummers.

In the early days, I never used to warm up or stretch. I'd have a nap before the show and then just get up there and start playing. When I got a little older, I started getting tweaks in my back and neck if I didn't warm up first—especially if the venue was outdoors. I remember a couple of shows in Helsinki in a hockey arena, where they put boards down over the ice. It was freezing, dude. When the huge stage lights would come on, the massive heat against the cold cymbals would cause them to crack with the slightest hit. Sometimes I wouldn't even need to hit a cymbal; being out in the cold, in the truck, and then coming in, the par lights would be enough to crack them without me even touching them. I learned the hard way that for those shows, I would have to rely on my crappy cymbals. I'd tell my tech, "Dude, don't use any of the good ones!"

That's pretty much the basic, Nick Menza 101 course in how I did what I did and what I do now. I always give Mustaine a lot of credit, ever since he told me, "I need you to know your shit. Play all the way through without anyone else playing. You don't know your parts from beginning to end, by yourself, without hearing anyone else, then you don't really know the songs. I need you to *know* the songs. If you're halfway through and the lead guitarist is just coming up on his solo and all the monitors go out and you can't hear shit, you'd better be able to play through as if nothing had happened and come out the other side perfectly. The audience should never be able to tell there was anything wrong because monitors would be a guide, not a lifeline."

That may sound obvious, but I'd never been told that explicitly before. I always played along with records, and I always learned the songs I was playing in bands. I made it my mission to know everybody's part of the songs, not just my own, so that I had the ability to pick up any point in any song and play with or without anyone else. That was awesome! I prided myself on it. Sure, I make mistakes—everybody does! Sometimes shit happens. You can't stress about mistakes, however, or you'll spiral into an abyss that will truly fuck you up. And you can't trip on what it sounds like on stage, because it's going to suck most times.

Speaking of being on stage, having chops is what should get you there, but it's still pretty hard to be cool if you don't look cool. It's a fact. Hair, clothes, attitude and your relationship with the audience—standing up, twirling sticks, pointing them with a rabid snarl, whatever is your deal—is all important. You're a big part of the show. People are there to *see* you play. You have to be adaptable and look the part for the gig. If you're decked out in black leather and piercings and tattoos, cool. But don't expect that audition for Shania Twain to go too well. You should look cool, obviously, and you have to be comfortable and air conditioned—cool in every way. And pay attention to where in the world you're playing. I never thought of this before it happened to me, but if you're anywhere above 3,000 feet elevation, you might notice the show wears you out a more quickly. The first time I played Red Rocks in Colorado, I didn't know what the deal was. I just couldn't catch my breath. I was tiring out well before I should have been. Then somebody told me it was the altitude—which, at 6,500 feet has, like, 20 percent less oxygen to breathe than at sea level. For a Megadeth show? Are you kidding me? I had the paramedics give me a quick hit of oxygen here and there between songs. Ripe!

Always, always, always be listening to music, unless you're playing it! I listen to any music, but of course I like it heavy. Right now in my car I have Meshuggah, Lamb of God, Periphery, Porcupine Tree, Gojira, and Symphony X. I like to check out my competition! I'm kidding. Actually, I seem to be into anything by any metal band coming out of Sweden. I don't know what they put in the water over there. Those guys from those bands are among my favorite drummers right now. I listen to music that moves me. If it makes the hair on my arm stand up, I'm going to listen to it. If my body goes, "Whoa! Awesome, dude!" then it's for me. If I hear music for the first time, and it makes me want to go get on the drums and play along with it, then it's probably pretty good. If I don't want to go play drums to it, then chances are it's not any good, or to my taste. It can be any kind of music—from hip-hop to jazz, from funk to R&B. I play to whatever's grooving.

As with every instrument, it's not what you play as much as the spaces you leave between what you do play. Every hit matters. They all need to be there. They all need to be a certain velocity. Anybody can play a million miles an hour, and there's no room for error because there isn't room for anything. It's just a big blur.

What makes really rad players and drummers is the space they leave in between what they play. What makes you great is knowing where to leave the space and when to play something simple. You can't fill every hole and make it sound great. I made it a point to play songs exactly as they were. Then I would play to make it better, in the ballpark phrasing of where you play everything, knowing where to play and where not to. Some beats are cliché for a reason, and you need to know what that reason is. That's part of building the basic vocabulary of drumming. I think of it like a person who reads a lot of books and one who doesn't. The more music you listen to, the more music's going to invade your thoughts. But when you're playing, if you start over-thinking it, it's going to suck because you'll lose the flow.

Got all that? Easy, huh?

One of the infinite gifts of being a father is getting to introduce Nicholas and Donte to music. Zeppelin, Rush, Sabbath, classical, jazz, pop, rock—everything I can get them to try out. They give me an excuse to listen to it all over again. Nicholas was hilarious as a baby. He loved Sabbath. He'd start to cry if Britney Spears came on, but a little Sabbath and he went right to sleep. He's definitely a rock dude. He doesn't want to listen to any of that pop stuff!

I'll give anything a chance, and I'm always happy to be surprised. I really like this girl, Kimbra, from New Zealand. She's a mix of pop with classic R&B, jazz, and rock. You can hear a little Prince, Björk, and Jeff Buckley in what she does. She's artsy and eclectic. I like to jam out to her songs because a lot of them don't have drums, and I like to see what I can do.

I encourage every drummer to pick up at least one other instrument. If you've ever been annoyed by a guitar or bass player yelling at you because you're too loud, too fast, or too slow, it really helps if you can play an instrument along with another drummer so you can yell at them too! Playing drums, you overcome a lot of the obstacles with instruments that are rhythm instruments. If you've got rhythm, it's pretty much easy to play guitar or bass or keyboards. Basically, what I'm doing is playing drums on everything I play. Whether it's guitar or bass, I treat it like a drum.

To be as good as you can be, you need to know what it's like in any position in the band. It's about listening. You will understand other instruments and the players. Then it will be *you* saying, "Oh! I get it! Dude, you're playing too loud. You're playing too fast!"

Believe me, it's the sort of thing that can make the difference between an amateur and a pro. Pros play well with others. I play guitar a lot, and I like to take songs like Rihanna's song "Stay" that this guy Mikky Ekko wrote for piano and vocals and make a heavy metal song out of it. Take a song off of YouTube, redo it, and put it back up on YouTube. I did it with Christina Aguilera's song "My Body." For a contest, her record company put all the stems up there. I took them, redid all the instruments, put in my voice along with her voice and put it back up there. It's fun! I called it the "Call Me" mix! (I'm still waiting for the call. Ha!)

I get asked all the time to rate drummers. There are the Top Gods, of course: Buddy, Peart, Bonham, and Gene Krupa, who Peart has said "was the first rock drummer."

I don't play like Stewart Copeland or Bill Bruford, but not many can. They are sonic artists, man, with unbelievable finesse.

When it comes to the world's most reliable, solid drummers, you don't have to look further than Jim Keltner, Steve Gadd, and some of the early cats like Jerry Allison. John "JR" Robinson has carried on their tradition. Moe Tucker was really cool and one of the leading chick drummers of the late '60s and '70s. Huge respect there, because she made it in a field that's hard for anyone to get ahead in. Check out Cindy Blackman who can lay down a groove that almost nobody can touch. It ain't my thing, but Earl Young invented the disco beat, and he was the human drum machine as far as I am concerned. Every great drummer out there who plays hard and heavy owes Earl Hudson. He is hardcore!

Levon Helm, Kenny Aronoff, Mick Fleetwood, Bill Ward, Max Weinberg, Matt Cameron, Alex Van Halen, Dave Lombardo; Chuck Flores—you're a fool if you don't study them and take away what they're best at. And always listen to the jazz greats like Buddy, Joe Morello, and Krupa. Doesn't matter if you don't like jazz. Black Sabbath's co-founder and original drummer Bill Ward was schooled in that shit. Look what it did for him.

Meshuggah's Tomas Haake and Rammstein's Christoph Schnieider are the best at what they do. And I'll always have to hand it to the nearly-naked, gravity-defying Tommy Lee. He's one of our greatest showmen.

When I think of a dude who can swing probably better than anyone, me included, it's Steve Jordan. Dave Grohl is a fucking monster. I don't know him, but he seems like one of the coolest dudes on the planet.

At first, I wasn't into all this social media stuff, but I've come around. You can work that like nothing else. Do all the media you can. Whether it's social media, which has revolutionized publicity, or online media or print—do 'em. They work.

Years ago, I told my publicist, Nancy, "You know what? I won't turn down any press. I don't care if it's a fanzine, college magazine, college radio; whatever. I'll do it." She said, "Ok."

She did! "Nancy, ah, there are fifteen interviews tomorrow! What the hell?"

She said, "Well, you told me you wouldn't turn down any press."

"Guess not."

I can't afford to. The people that do fanzines are awesome. Remember, these are your fans. It's like, "Hey, relax, don't be nervous. Someday you might be the editor of *Billboard* and you'll go, 'Nick Menza gave me my first interview, and he was very cool. And I appreciate that. So, I'm gonna give him this article in *Billboard*.'"

And I'm like, "Thank you."

There are people I've run across that are working in big positions who started out way down the ladder, and they've said, "Yeah, you were really cool to me back then."

I don't think that there's any press that's too big or too small or anyone's more important than anyone else. It's all press. I don't care what they're saying, just as long as it's there. I post shit and am shocked at how many hits I get and from where—countries I've never even heard of sometimes.

That's the power of music. If music doesn't take you somewhere then it's not doing its job. And if it does, music doesn't lie. Whatever the song is, whatever genre, it's got to have a vibe that carries you to some place you've never been before, or some place where you're comfortable, safe, and feel loved. It's got to be a real song that's got meaning to it. Not some bullshit rap or hook, but meaningful words and a meaningful melody that causes you to come away from it changed. The first time you hear it, if you walk away humming it, it's a hit. Of course, there have been times where the first time I've listened to something I've thought "This song sucks" and then all of a sudden, I go, "Wait a minute!"

I've always joked that I want to have one hit song of my own, one of those tunes that people get sick of hearing—the kind of song chicks request at their weddings. I want to hear people say, "Stop playing that! I hate it! That song sucks!" That would be cool.

Here's a test. Pay attention to the first song you hear after you wake up in the morning. I don't care what it is. If it's good, it will be with you all day.

In Megadeth, we'd complain to the record companies that we wanted to be on morning rotation. They were like, "Who wants to be on morning rotation?"

Our fans are up all night partying, and they're up in the morning going to work, sitting on the freeway. Those are the people we wanted to hit. We also wanted morning rotation to pull in some crossover fans.

Another simple but golden rule: if you don't repeat the chorus, your song doesn't have a chance of doing anything at all. When people remember the chorus of your song, chances are they'll go and buy it. Producer Max Norman used to say to us, "Don't bore us; get to the fucking chorus."

You've got to love the music business because sometimes it doesn't love you, and you're left with whatever devices you have available.

Welcome to the world of drumming, Nick Menza style!

It's hard work, but it's worth it. Check this out. Scientists say that drumming will catalyze your white-blood-cell count, which in turn increases your body's immunity to disease. In terms of rhythm, learning how to speed up or slow down a song's time signature can make you better at thinking on your feet in everything else in life. Rhythm also makes you a better dancer and a bear in bed with your lady. Really!

Finally, focusing on drumming has been proven to also enhance your everyday cognitive skills, which means your IQ, dude.

Here endeth the Menza, Mensa lesson!

"THAT TERRIBLE NIGHT"

May 21, 2016.

"We did the soundcheck, and it was a laugh a minute," Chris Poland says. "And then Nick went out with Gary (Nick's drum tech) to get something to eat.

"When we started the gig that night, Nick was playing better than anybody I've ever played with. He'd gotten so in shape from all the bike riding—two or three miles a day up and down a mountain. He'd lost twenty-five to thirty pounds. There were no drugs or anything. He was into his health. All that guy did was make cajóns all day, make music, and invent stuff. And ride his mountain bike.

"He turned me on to so much shit. I gotta tell you this story about the monitors he built for his studio. A guy from Speaker City came to hear them and said, 'I don't know how these are even possible; there are no standing waves anywhere.' I know these guys, and they're total snobs. If your speakers suck, they'll tell you. Nick was a genius. Everything he touched. That's how everybody felt about him. Except Mustaine. Dave was so jealous of him. Nick became the real star of Megadeth. Nick would tell me these stories that would make me so upset about Mustaine being so petty, freezing Nick's money and stuff. It didn't need to happen. The things Mustaine did to that man. There was not a hateful bone in Nick's body. He just wouldn't hold grudges."

"That terrible night was the best," Pag says. "He was playing drums like I've never heard before."

"I was just like, wow, and I looked over at Pag, and we looked at each other and smiled," says Poland. "It was relentless. By the second song my face was dripping all over my guitar. After the first song Nick asked me, 'Are you ok?'"

"I was soaking wet. 'What is going on with you?' I asked him. He just laughed, tuned his snare a little bit, and we went on to the next song. He'd never played that way before. The coolest thing about Nick was he'd make it sound simple. That's what changed us. All of a sudden, we had muscle and taste, instead of just eclecticism. We went from jazzy to jazzy Led Zeppelin playing in 9-7. It was pummeling.

"He kept asking me if I was ok. It was funny. Then at the end of the third song he looked at Pag, and they winked at each other. He adjusted his high-hat, put his hands on his knees, and leaned into the monitor. I thought he was messing with me. He used to call me The Old Man. I said, 'Come on, dude, don't fuck around.' But Nick didn't move. I knew then that he wasn't playing a joke on us. He was leaning up against the monitor with his eyes open and wasn't moving. I freaked out, threw my guitar down and, as I ran around the drums, yelled for somebody to call a paramedic."

"When we finished the third song, Chris and I were already hot and tired and sweating," Pag says. "Nick was really pushing us and was having a great time. I turned around, and we winked at each other. I went back to the mic. Then I turned around and Nick was up against my monitor. I said, 'You all right?' He lunged back violently and fell behind the kit sort of like he had a seizure. Everybody started rushing the stage, knocking over cymbals. People immediately jumped on top of him and started mouth to mouth and pounding on his chest."

So many people rushed the stage so quickly to help, including an off-duty EMT, that Pags was surrounded and didn't have enough room to take off his bass.

"The paramedic from the audience said he had a pulse. The ambulance got there right away, and they wouldn't give up, man," Pag recalls. "They worked on him for at least forty-five minutes."

"The paramedics went through three (defibrillator) batteries," says Poland. "By the second battery, I couldn't watch any more. His ribs were broken from all the work they were doing trying to bring him back. I left. I was fucking crushed. I think they were saying they had a pulse just so they could get him out of there and so people wouldn't beat the shit of out them."

Poland and Pag left the room and went outside to join Nick's mother and sister, who had arrived from their nearby homes.

"I went outside to see Rose and Donia—the paramedics wouldn't let them into the club where they were working on Nick," Pag says. "There was so much chaos since everyone from the club had been taken outside. When they put him on the gurney and brought him out the crowd was cheering him on, 'You're gonna be ok, Nick!'

"They took him away and sometime later Donia called my wife's phone and said, 'He's gone.' And that was it."

Rumors surfaced shortly thereafter that Nick knew he had a bad heart and that he was in need of surgery.

"It's absolutely not true that he needed surgery or anything," Donia says. "It was never the case. Nick was in great shape. I'm an avid bike rider and I couldn't keep up with him. I said, 'Nick, you're fifty, you have to listen to your body. Take a couple of days off and not play the drums or ride your bike.'

"Nick said he can't take it easy, since people expect him to play hard and loud or 'I won't be the drummer everybody wants to see.'

"Those rumors bother me. But I know what really happened. Heart disease is a silent killer; it doesn't show up on your regular physical, no signs. It's the first thing I'd say to anybody, get a stress test and ultra sound, a CAT scan.

"He didn't have the smallest hint he was going to die soon."

Poland and Pag agree, saying Nick was at the height of energy, enthusiasm, and optimism.

"One of my lasting memories of Nick is from one of our first gigs," Pag says. "I was moving my gear, struggling with my cabinets, and he said, 'That's not right, you've paid your dues. I got a guy who will take care of all that. You're never going to have to lift gear again.' Nick said I needed new wheels on my rack, and he showed up the next day with a screwdriver and a drill and new wheels. That's the kind of guy Nick was. We hit it off immediately and became really close really fast, which is something I'll never forget.

"There were people who saw every gig we did, and they said that last night was out of control—the best they'd ever seen us. This is it, all the things building, buzz going on, going to Europe, it was time to break out, and we were chomping at the bit. We'd never have been able to open for anybody because nobody would want to play with us. We'd just terrorize them!

"I just knew from the first day I played with Nick it was going to be something really special, and that night it really was. I'm glad it was taped. I've listened to it. That was the night it all really came together. It's so devastating to see where things ended up. But everything happens for a reason, whether we know what it is or not."

Nick's family, friends and fans have been so active on social media in the year since Nick died, and I hope they'll continue to be, telling stories of the man we all love so much.

I've combed through the dozens of interviews and stories and pulled out a few that I'd be remiss for not including.

Nick, as he said in the beginning, never kept a tour diary or journal. He lived in the moment, trying to never look back in regrets or too far into the future with unreasonable expectations. But he believed in magic, always—something he told me was one of the never-ending gifts he cherished from being Nicholas and Donte's father.

His lifelong friend Juan Alvarez was on the road with Megadeth for two tours as the band videographer and running buddy of Nick's.

"We met pretty early on," Juan recalls. "Maybe about fifteen or sixteen. We started our first band together with a guy named Mike Max on guitar. We played all these house parties and played the whole *Song Remains the Same* and then all of *2112*. It was a pretty amazing time. As friends, we were all so tight and so close. I'm sure it was pretty pathetic at first, but I know we got good. We were pretty tough on ourselves, trying to imitate our idols; so getting the songs right was critical. We'd be down rehearsing in the basement at Nick's house, every day, playing "Dazed and Confused" or whatever. We were so nuts about it that Don bought Mike a bow for his guitar so he could imitate Jimmy Page even more. It was beautiful.

"One of the great things that I'll always cherish is the music of the Menza family. There was music playing *all* the time—jazz, classical, and, upstairs in Nick's room, rock 'n' roll."

One remembrance that I want to include is from Nick's one-time partner-in-rhythm, David Ellefson.

For context, Nick and I reached out to Dave Mustaine and David Ellefson on several occasions from the beginning of this project. Ellefson has been helpful, polite, and respectful every time we've spoken. At first, after Nick's passing, Mustaine made some beautiful public gestures and tributes to Nick, but he has declined to participate in this book. Most recently, he began hanging up on me, sending me nasty texts, and he now tells reporters that "Out of respect to the dead, I'm not gonna talk bad about (Nick)."

Ah well. Can't say he wasn't asked. I've resisted editorializing, but I am not going to resist pointing out that this is a man who still, as of this writing, hasn't had the class to send a condolence card and whose only phone call to the family was to try to entice Nick's Mom into some kind of business deal. As Nick would say, "Dude, what are you, new?"

For his part, Ellefson has warmly helped shape the tone of fond remembrances of Nick.

We first spoke when Nick and I began the book, as Nick was returning to the music world with sessions and workshops, which would lead to him playing with James LoMenzo and Chris Poland and, finally, Ohm. There had already been considerable press about the book being in the works.

"The fans are stoked that Nick's back on the radar," Junior told me from his home in Phoenix in our first conversation. "His new manager (Rob) is the right kind of guy for Nick. He's ballsy, and he's the guy to help Nick get back in the spotlight."

Junior recalled that meeting Nick for the first time was something that would always stand out in his memory. "Our guitar tech at the time was Gumby, John Goodwin. He knew Nick and told us that, 'He's a real firecracker.'

"My first memory of Nick, the first time I met him, we were starting the So Far, So Good...So What! Tour in 1988, and we did a little short run of club shows on the West Coast before we were going to start up with Ronnie James Dio in Providence, Rhode Island. Nick was brought in by our sound man, Neil Shaffer. He was brought in as a drum tech but also as an understudy for our drummer at the time, Chuck Belher. We were sure of Nick's abilities. He didn't say a lot, but he was cocky, bold."

Junior remembers the first soundcheck with Nick in the crew. "Me and Chuck were at this soundcheck and Dave couldn't get down in time, so we started playing, and Nick steps up to Dave's mic and starts singing "Peace Sells!" I thought, *You are one bold motherfucker!*

"That's the one thing on Dave's stage: *nobody* talks through that mic. And here's Nick up there throwing down and singing. I thought, 'There's going to be hell to pay for that somewhere down the line.' I don't know if any of us told Dave about that, but the next ten years was sure a lot of Nick being Nick!"

By the following year, it was time "to make a drummer change," Ellefson recalls.

"Nick was our man. Dave told me to go audition Nick at this small rehearsal hall just west of the Burbank airport in the North Hollywood. I was usually the guy who did this, and we went into the room, just me and Nick and drums. It was a green Pearl kit, and he came in early and was so excited. The first song we played was "Mechanics," which was a song that Dave had from his Metallica days. I remember Nick was so pumped and full of energy, we started at one tempo and barely got to the second chorus and we'd picked up by about 40 BPM! Nick just really understood the energy of metal and understood the performance and showbiz aspect of it.

"Nick showed that he really wanted the gig and would do anything for it. I used to go over to Nick's apartment and hang out with him. It was a revolving door of his friends, of his high school buddies. People would come and hang out and grab a beer out of the fridge or a Coke or something. It was very casual and an easy hang. It reminded me of growing up on a farm in Minnesota. There was [sic] always people coming over. When I moved to L.A. that never happened; that was so not the culture of living in the city. But at Nick's apartment, there were always people coming over.

"Nick wasn't all that patient, which I understand. He was waiting for that door (to the Megadeth drum job) to open. I said to him, 'Here's one thing: you've got a personality like Dave Mustaine, which is great to have, but there's only room for one Dave in Megadeth.'

"I think Nick and his hunger and drive is what got him the gig and what makes him such a celebrated member of the Megadeth history. Yet at the same time too many cooks in the kitchen spoils the broth, as they say. And that relationship of Nick in Megadeth always took it right to the line, always, and again, it's why I think the energy was so great for the band when he was in it; and it's what made the creative output so high and the quality of what we did so high. Because sometimes you just have to be the sideman in the band, and sometimes you need to be the rock star in the band. Nick probably had a harder time accepting the sideman role. He was just wired to be a front man. He could sing; he could play guitar. Nick was a really creatively expressive guy, probably growing up under the iron fist of his father, Don, who was a really strict discipli-narian, but who really understood the music business. I remember Nick telling me that Don would always have these discussions with him and tell him, 'Look, it's Mustaine's band. You need to show up, do what he says, and be his guy.' And Nick, I think all of us when we're young we look at the posters on our wall of our favorite rock bands and think, *Oh, it's four guys all together, it's a gang, they all get to do what they want*, and then you get to this point in your adulthood where you've been in enough bands that you get into one that's really working and you realize that those bands have a leader and there's a vision and you have to get behind that vision and get behind that leader in order for it to work.

"If Nick ever had a struggle with anything, it was being in something so outlaw and crazy as a rock band and having to still submit to some kind of authority. I think that was the part with Nick that came the hard-est for him, just because of his propensity to naturally be in the spotlight and be the leader himself. There's [sic] not a lot of people who can do that. I think quite honestly that's one of the reasons a lot of the lineup changes happen. We all want to have that great gig, but not all people realize that gig comes with a lot more than just the notes, you know? Don

Menza realizes that, for sure, and he's got that drive and that fire because Don's also a wonderful artist and a wonderful musician, and somehow [he] found that balance and is able to play under the biggest names in the business while also able to have his own creative outlet. Any of us who've been successful in Megadeth over the years have had to find that. And there comes a point where you can only fight that internally for so long and my opinion is, just knowing Nick as a friend and seeing him at his most vivacious and healthy and then seeing him frustrated and unhappy at the end of his time with Megadeth, I think that dynamic is one that he could not really come to terms with at that point in his life.

"All of us have felt that over the years, and I guess me maybe more than most, have a soft spot for Nick and understood that about Nick; and knowing him as a friend first and then knowing him as a band member, we were able to keep a friendship. Even though it's been distant, there's still a fondness and friendship even though in our professional lives we've had twists and turns over the years. Both have included and not included Megadeth."

When Nick joined Chris Poland and Pag in their band Ohm, Ellefson again reached out to talk about him.

"I think it's exciting," he said. "I think it's a good part of the whole overall package. I think God's lining Nick back up and getting him suited up and ready for battle, getting back on the front lines in a way that he's able to handle it now. I think it's just a great way to come back into the game, you know what I mean?"

After Nick passed away, Ellefson offered some kind memories.

"Nick was a constant comedy act. He was so fun. Just walking up on stage and stepping up on his drum riser and holding his sticks up in the cross: 'The power of Christ compels you!' He'd quote *The Exorcist*, and you'd just look at him and smile. We were writing and rehearsing the *Youthanasia* record at a studio in Phoenix, and they had some artwork on the wall. He was into painting. I didn't quite get his paintings—they were a little abstract—but he was into it. He put a painting on the wall and wrote the price on it. A hundred grand! That was Nick's over-the-top bombast to just shock you, you know. And that's what made him so cool behind the drums. He brought such a great spirit to the band, such a fun era of heavy metal during the '90s when he was with us. I miss him."

Marty Friedman echoes Junior's thoughts, while having a deeper assessment of what made Nick the world-class drummer he was.

"Nick had a much more 'human' feel than most metal drummers," Friedman wrote to me in an email. "'Human' often means 'bad timing' in the case of drummers, but not in Nick's case. He was solid as a rock without having that 'machine-like' sound that many metal drummers have. Where the riff would call for 'metal drumming' Nick would put a 'rock' feel there, but [he would] play it so aggressively that it fools you into thinking it's metal. This is what gave Megadeth the mainstream appeal it got when he and I joined. If he would have played the typical metal beats at that time, Megadeth may have just fallen into the category of so many thrash bands of the day. His playing allowed even girls to enjoy our heavy music. It made it more accessible than it really was. The Megadeth drummers before Nick were very talented, but Nick was the first with mainstream appeal. He had rock-star charisma and good looks on top of his talent, and that is essential in the big leagues."

Which is why Friedman hired Nick to play drums on his first solo records.

"We definitely had the shorthand, and that is why I hired him. Before recording *Scenes*, I had just been on a massive tour with Megadeth, about 200 shows of furious thrashing every night. So I wanted a complete change of pace, as I'm sure Nick did. *Scenes* was done in a very unorthodox fashion. I meticulously recorded all the musical tracks first to a click track and recorded the drums last. Nick played to a completed full-band track. This is never done, and was experimental and quite risky on my part. Nick hit home runs on every track, bringing the previously very clinically played parts to life. He literally breathed life into the tracks on that album. Explaining this "backwards" recording process to most drummers would have been tedious, but Nick got it right away and absolutely owned the tracks. We did the same thing again on the *Introduction* album. I never did this process again with another drummer. I don't think anyone could top the tracks Nick did on those two albums.

"He would play bass and guitar, too. He also sang, and I thought it was a crime that he didn't sing in Megadeth because he had a truly fantastic rock voice. Big league. When it came to drums, he always wanted to put the challenging songs in the set list; he was always pushing us to be better.

"Our musicality was a bond right away. To be frank, I knew that Dave and David were thrash masters, but I didn't think they were so 'musical' back then. I knew that Nick had music in his soul and was not just a metal guy with fast feet. He grew up with music, and he seemed like a 'musician' rather than a 'thrash metal guy.' I could relate to that, as I was a musician first and thrasher second. Luckily, I had that 'thrash chromosome' so I could fit in with the band and relate to what they were trying to do, but when I got home I was probably listening to something totally different. I believe Nick was the same way, so we bonded that way early on."

Friedman says he had exactly the same experience recording with Nick's father, Don, who came in to play shakuhachi (a Japanese end-blown bamboo flute) on Friedman's *Introduction* record.

"I met Don several times and knew he was a world-class musician," says Friedman, "but I never thought I could get someone of his caliber on one of my records. Also, I didn't have flutes or saxes in my music back then. However, when he told me he played shakuhachi, I saw an opportunity, so I wrote a part for him to play on my song 'Bittersweet.' He nailed it in one take, and it was gorgeous."

Friedman says that he and Nick never had an opportunity to play any of his solo material together live, since their work in Megadeth was so consuming, and "I didn't start touring for my solo work until 2002. By that time we were both in separate circles. We didn't talk music too much, because we were doing music 24/7. We were both more interested in getting good food on the road. While all four of us in the band were foodies, so to speak, Nick was an outstanding cook, and he would often whip up some world-class Italian food for us like it was nothing. He had a huge talent for that, and all of us loved it when he cooked. Often Nick and I would search for the best Korean restaurants in whatever town we were in. In Megadeth, we would often hang out in pairs. Dave and I would hang, or David and I, or Nick and I. We would always do different things together. David and I would go clothes shopping a lot. Dave and I would grab pizza in New York the second we arrived. Nick and I would either find sushi or Korean food. Nick knew good food, and we would enjoy returning to places that we knew were good."

Friedman, who has lived in Japan for many years, wasn't in close contact with Nick—or anyone in the old Megadeth camp—but, he says, "I was as shocked as anyone else at the news. I had just seen him maybe a year prior to his passing when the four Megadeth members had a real nice dinner together after around fifteen years apart. We got together to discuss a possible reunion. That didn't happen, but the four of us together just shooting the shit will always be a fond memory for me. Nick was a real character in the best sense of the word—a world-class drummer, friend, and overall inspirational guy. Look at the way he played drums in the early Megadeth days. That is the way he attacked life. Full on, full power, and total abandon. He did not pussyfoot around on those drums. He played like a man. I miss the guy."

In the week after Nick's tragic passing, his family held a private memorial service at the home where he grew up and where so many of his friends hung out through their teen years. His family and dozens of friends and fellow musicians came to celebrate Nick's life, love, humor, humanity...and music.

Although Nick isn't here any longer, he's far from gone.

That's true for as long as we can hear his music, see his art, and experience his wit, wisdom and whimsy. He lives on in his family, Rose, Don, and Donia; and in his two spectacular sons, Nicholas and Donte.

LAST WORD

Shortly before he passed away, I asked Nick to look over his introduction for this book, as some time had passed between our first draft and the planned publication. A lot had happened in his life, including a second, final and failed Megadeth reunion.

No matter what was or is in the media, whether Nick was quoted accurately or not, just three weeks before he died he decided to "set the record straight and tell fans and the other guys in Megadeth how I really feel, now that we're not going back and forth in negotiations or playing our private stuff and feelings out in a public way."

Nick was angry, yet again, at how he'd been treated by Mustaine. Throughout his life after Megadeth, he was in a never-ending battle to get his royalties every few months; they were either forthcoming as required or held back by Mustaine for one reason or another. Within the passing of about a year since the *Rust In Peace* lineup reunion collapsed, Nick was again positive and seeing the bright side of things. He never lost hope that there would someday be at least a one-off reunion of the great Megadeth he and Marty remain most famous for. Nick never failed to praise Mustaine and emphasize all the wonderful things he learned from him in the studio, on the road, and as a musician. Nick said he was compelled to speak out publicly about his dissatisfactions about how things had spun out, "because people are always asking me when it's going to happen, and now, 'Dude, what happened? Why did you turn it down?'"

But he never gave up hope.

One statement I heard over and over again in the years I knew Nick and spoke with people who knew him is, "Nick's the nicest guy you'll ever meet; happy, always smiling, joking around, laughing."

It's true. He is. He was.

Nick's family and friends have had the measured consideration and reflection that time grants, at its own pace for each of us, perhaps, after suffering such a devastating loss. Fortunately, Nick and his sons Nicholas and Donte treasured ten days together just weeks before his passing. Now, Nick's family agrees that it's appropriate and illustrative of what a fine father he was to his two striking, intelligent, and wise-beyond-their-years sons to make public this text his eldest son Nicholas sent to his father's phone in the hours after learning of his Dad's passing, knowing Nick would never read it. Few would argue it's not an at-once heartbreaking and enlightening glimpse of the sort of man Nick is. What sort of father. And of his two sons.

"Ok you'll never see this, but I love you so much bro. So much. I couldn't have asked for a better Dad. I'm going to do my best to view life like you did, you tried to teach me how to view it while you were living, but I didn't listen. Now I am. The most painful thing is that you won't be here to see me change into a better man. But I know you'll always be with us. You taught me to smile through all the bullshit, cause there's always brighter day. You taught me when you put in good energy into the universe, good things come out of it. For one reason or another, the universe wanted you, and you wanted to be part of the universe. You got your wish, you recently told me you wanted to eventually move to Alaska, to be yourself, to live your life the way you wanted, even though you did anything you wanted anyway. In a way, you got your Alaska bro. You're in your own land now. Nothing could have stopped that. What's making me get through this is that I know you're here with us for a while, I felt your energy comforting me last night, things have happened that are unexplainable. As well, you were so at peace with every-thing, I'm glad you left us with you being in the right mind, a higher thinking. I'm so blessed to have been your son. I will watch over the family for you. As long as you promise to always be up there watch-ing over the family, and by family I literally mean everyone in our family, from Cali, Washington and where ever there is a Menza and Ontiveros. I really am glad that you knew you would die doing what you loved, you were and are a true badass bro. I will never forget you bro. I hope that this only brings the families closer together, I will make sure that it does bro, know that. And know, my last promise to you is that I will grow up, being successful at whatever I do in life, I'll bring pride to the Menza name, I will pick up the Menza torch, I will do everything I can to make sure you are remembered and that your message is told. I will not grow up a fuck up. I promise. I won't mess around, I'll stay on my studies. I'll be the man you saw in me. I love you Dad, Rest in paradise. When I hear the thunder roar, I'll always think of you. I know you won't be quiet, dead or alive. Love you, Dad."

—Nicholas Sebastian Menza, 15
May 22, 2016

"And that concludes our taco-time show tip for today, on the universe, tacos—and a flat Earth."

—The last words spoken by Nick on camera.

ACKNOWLEDGMENTS

This book would not have been possible without the generous time, spirit, energy and deep love of Rose, Don and Donia Menza, Nick's boys, Nicholas and Donte, and their mother, Terri.

Nick's friends and/or bandmates were key to telling this story and then amending it after Nick's passing. John "Gumby" Goodwin, Chris Poland, Robertino "Pag" Pagliari, Dave "Junior" Ellefson, Marty Friedman, James LoMenzo, Chris Grady, (the late, wonderful) Darwin Ballard, Juan Alvarez, Allen Hall, Kelle Rhodes, Christian Nesmith, Anthony Gallo, Iki Levy, Neil Shaffer, Frank Conte. If I am forgetting anyone who helped Nick and me immeasurably with this book, please forgive me.

Nick's manager, Robert Bolger, was one of Nick's biggest supporters and believers, ever, and their professional relationship was one of the most solid, trusting, and respectful I've ever witnessed in the music business. Rob continues to hold Nick's torch high, and bless him for it. He and Rose, even more than I, have been the target of a whole lot of nasty from some corners of the Megadeth camp for a long time now. On the other hand, I'm grateful for the kind considerations of various present and former Megadeth crew and staff members who spoke to me and shared beautiful memories of Nick, on the condition I didn't use their names.

I extend my personal gratitude to my agents Mel Berger at William Morris Endeavor for his years of support and James Fitzgerald at the James Fitzgerald Agency for helping with this project. I lead a blessed literary life and Jacob Hoye at Post Hill Press has been the finest editor I've had the honor of working with. I'm in his debt, and I yield to the stark fact that any errors or omissions in this book are mine alone.

ACKNOWLEDGMENTS

I am doubly grateful to my wife Kris and the kiddos Jordan, Rocco, Robert, Josephine, and Squire William who had to endure more than a few selfish "writer-boy" times as I completed this project.

Finally, I would like to say to Nick's incredible fans all over the world, an untold number of whom showed vast enthusiasm, encouragement, and support for this book from its inception: Nick worshipped every one of you, and even in his darkest hours, he never let slip his gratitude for your attention, your ears, and your love.

J. Marshall Craig

PHOTO CREDITS

PHOTO CREDITS

Page 126: Nick Menza Personal Archive

Page 133: Courtesy Iki Levy/Soultone Cymbals

Page 138: Brooks Ayola

Page 147: Nick Menza Personal Archive

Page 153: Nick Menza Personal Archive

Page 161: Courtesy Iki Levy/Soultone Cymbals

Page 167: Courtesy Iki Levy/Soultone Cymbals

Page 180: Nick Menza Estate

Page 193: Nick Menza

INSERT

Page 1: Don Menza

Page 2 Top: Nick Menza Personal Archive

Page 2 Bottom: Don Menza

Page 3 Top: Don Menza

Page 3 Bottom left and right: Nick Menza Personal Archive

Page 4: Nick Menza Personal Archive

Page 5 Top: Courtesy of Dawn Brumley

Page 5 Bottom: Nick Menza Personal Archive

Page 6: Kristin Hughes-Craig

Page 7: SceneFour Inc.

Page 8 Top: Courtesy of Gabriel Olsen/FilmMagic

Page 8 Bottom: Nick Menza Estate

ABOUT THE AUTHOR

J. Marshall Craig is the author of, and contributor to, more than a dozen books and collected writings. These include his novel *Eh Mail*; his historical non-fiction book on World War I, *You're Lucky If You're Killed*; the environmental book *Growing A Better America: Smart, Strong and Sustainable* (with Chuck Leavell); and memoirs with Eric Burdon (*Don't Let Me Be Misunderstood*), Chuck Leavell (*Between Rock and A Home Place*), Damion Young (*Guilty By Association*), and John Rocker (*Scars & Strikes*). His work appears in several literary collections with Tom Wolfe, Hunter S. Thompson, Jack Kerouac, and others (*The Outlaw Bible of American Literature*); Hell's Angels founder Sonny Barger, Che Guevara, and others (*She's A Bad Motorcycle*) and former CNN talk show host Larry King (*Remember Me When I'm Gone*).

A resident of Southern California for most of his adult life, Canadian-born Craig now lives, writes, and plays guitar on Cape Cod, Massachusetts.